The Professional Secretary's Handbook

MANAGEMENT SKILLS

John Spencer and Adrian Pruss

First edition for the United States and Canada
published 1997 by Barron's Educational Series, Inc.

First published in Great Britain under the title
The Professional Secretary Volume 2.

© 1995 by John Spencer and Adrian Pruss

By arrangement with Cassel plc
Wellington House, 125 Strand
London WC2R, 0BB, England

All inquiries should be addressed to:
Barron's Educational Series, Inc.
250 Wireless Boulevard
Hauppauge, New York 11788

Library of Congress Catalog Card No. 96-42919
International Standard Book No. 0-7641-0024-6

Library of Congress Cataloging-in-Publication Data
Spencer, John (John Leslie), 1954–
    [Professional secretary. v. 2. Management skills]
    The professional secretary's handbook. Management skills / John
Spencer and Adrian Pruss.
        p.   cm.
    Originally published as vol. 2 of: The professional secretary / John
Spencer and Adrian Pruss. London : New York : Cassell, © 1995.
    Includes Index.
    ISBN 0-7641-0024-6
    1. Secretaries. 2. Business communication. 3. Office management.
I. Pruss, Adrian. II. Title.
HF5547.S724   1997
651.3'74—dc20   96-42919
                                                                  CIP

PRINTED IN THE UNITED STATES OF AMERICA

987654321

Contents

Part 1 Managing the Secretarial Team

Part 3 **The Lone Arranger**

Foreword

A secretary is a manager, but is seldom given the credit for being so. She, or he, is the oil that lubricates the grinding cogs and wheels of corporate organizations to ensure a smooth running of day-to-day business. The backbone of any organization, the secretary's management skills must be developed to an impeccable and excellent standard, but all too often, when it comes to personal development and management training, the secretary is the office's forgotten breed.

During my time as the editor of *Office Secretary* magazine, the largest circulation secretarial business journal in the United Kingdom, I found a remarkable trainer and presenter, empathic to the secretary's struggle for recognition and eagerness to better her status at work. And together John Spencer and I created management level training to offer a personal development program just for secretaries. John's background in training at blue chip company director and manager levels gave him a clear understanding of what kind of support these people constantly need from their secretaries, and his expertise in good management methods lent itself to the creation of a highly relevant, informative and practical training program for the background managers, the frontliners, the miracle workers—the secretaries.

This book is the second of two by John Spencer and his colleague Adrian Pruss that are the offspring of those highly successful courses, now run by John and Adrian's training company, APW. The first volume focuses on communications skills, a basic and vital ingredient for all secretaries, and covers written and telephone communication, meetings organization and participation, and assertiveness skills. This, the second book, is the management skills volume, a crucially important tutor and guide to understanding what good management is, and how to apply it.

Within its pages you will find a lively and refreshing presentation of time management techniques, with a particular sympathy for and understanding of the often delicate circumstances, and of managing the secretarial team, where a senior secretary must exercise all the skills of an office manager to run an efficient administration team, from task training to counseling and maintaining discipline. The book will also guide you through important rules and methods of good communication, and show you how to use positive influencing skills to achieve your work requirements. Not forgetting that the secretary is a lone tower, whether in a large or a small organization, the authors devote part of the book to the "Lone Arranger," the secretary who has to cope with everything without a support team.

What makes this book different from the rest? Spencer and Pruss irreverently toss unusable, standard, management myths and fables into the bin and replace them with reality. We know that the secretary's role is a particularly delicate one. Having to deal with often unprofessional colleagues, or those who expect the impossible, call for distinctive management handling skills—and there are simple, straightforward techniques, practical, real-life solutions, ideas, and methods for every secretary to try. No management myth and fables here.

What Spencer and Pruss present in a lively, fun-to-read, and energetic style is a means for moving forward and upward in your career. They arm you with the means to deal with people effectively. They offer you several ways to gain recognition for your vital role by acquiring new skills and showing the rest of the management what you are capable of.

This book will unleash your potential, and awaken the dormant greatness within.

Onay Faiz
Former Editor and Training Coordinator, *Office Secretary*
Currently Training Development Manager, The Training Network

About the Authors

John Spencer

Specialist trainer and lecturer in management development skills; specialist lecturer in accountancy, finance, and taxation. Consultant, lecturer, and trainer to the financial services sector. Organized, developed, and delivered the "Executive Secretaries into Management" training courses for delegates from over 200 leading U.K. companies. As well as industrial and commercial experience, he is retained by clients in the entertainment and media industries. Well-known contributor to magazine, radio, and TV media on a variety of "personal development" subjects. Author of many business books, and co-author with Adrian Pruss of *Managing Your Team* and *How to Implement Change in Your Company*.

Adrian Pruss

City-trained accountant. Prior to founding APW Training, positions held included academic and boardroom appointments. Now a management consultant specializing in organizational review, cost reduction, and change programs. A management development consultant and trainer for multinational, industrial, and commercial organizations in Europe, the United States, and Africa. Co-author with John Spencer of the books *Managing Your Team* and *How to Implement Change in Your Company*.

About APW Training

APW Training, the company run by John Spencer and Adrian Pruss, is at the forefront of training that brings management level skills and approaches to secretarial development. Over the past four years, APW Training has delivered its courses to secretaries from over 200 leading companies worldwide.

Introduction

The secretary's success books contain the core skills needed by any secretary seeking promotion or a move into management. The skills outlined represent the most demanded courses in training programs run by the authors over 15 years. In the past four years, we have been delivering these courses to secretaries from over 200 of the top U.K. and international companies. The courses have addressed the real-world problems and issues of the modern secretary. Exit reports from those courses have been 100 percent positive. Typical comments made have been:

Dealt with the subject of time management in a straightforward and realistic way.

Course trainer was very good—he obviously understood the problems of meetings.

This was a constructive, positive course.

Excellent value, comfortable but speedy pace.

Very interesting and informative.

A good day with plenty of ideas to take back to the office.

The course was of a very high standard.

Never a dull moment. Interest maintained at all times.

Most enjoyable, entertaining, but most of all interesting and enormous help to progression in the 1990s.

An excellent day. I gained a great deal of knowledge.

Further feedback from delegates on the courses has indicated that they are able to use the material for career progress, job enhancement, and improving relationships with their bosses and others.

The training objectives of the courses, which are reflected in these books, meet the varied needs of secretaries who want to:

- make more of their jobs;
- acquire skills that will take them into executive secretary/administrative assistant standard;
- break the "glass ceiling" and move into management.

The Professional Secretary comes in two volumes:

Volume 1: Communication Skills covers:

- the most successful skills for meetings, minutes, and agendas;
- the most successful skills for using the telephone;
- the most successful skills for persuasive writing;
- the most successful assertiveness program.

Volume 2: Management Skills covers:

- the most successful skills of team management;
- the most successful skills of time management;
- the most successful skills of solo management;
- the most successful skills of motivation, influencing, and communication.

By following the very practical guidance in these two volumes, you will enhance your work, gain greater enjoyment from your work, and increase your chances of promotion ahead of less skilled colleagues.

Enjoy the books, enjoy your future work, and enjoy the promotion that will soon be coming your way.

Note: To avoid the awkwardness of *he/she* references, masculine and feminine pronouns are used alternatively throughout the book.

PART 1

Managing the
Secretarial Team

Companies are more and more recognizing the value of the synergy of teams. A group of people together can achieve more than each of them separately. Secretarial teams are already becoming an organized support in many companies. Whether you are, or might one day, be part of or leader of such a team, or whether you are the senior secretary in your department, this section contains the important information that you need. It covers: leadership of the team or department; understanding the varied characteristics of the members of your team, and how to balance them for maximum performance; dealing with stress in yourself and others; how to encourage your team to learn; interviewing; staff appraisal; counseling in the workplace; workstation common sense; and avoidance of RSI (repetitive strain injury).

Leadership

Our organization wants us to be more effective but what am I supposed to do about it?

This question was voiced by a secretarial team leader at a residential weekend on team building in 1994. No doubt this question has been voiced by team leaders and managers throughout the United Kingdom for many years. But the question only creates other questions:

- What are the qualities of leadership?
- What actions should a leader perform?

Any team of secretaries will expect its team leader to have qualities, and these may have to vary with the situation. There is not, however, a standard mix of qualities to make the perfect leader in all situations. One management writer, Feinberg, studied leadership and identified some common ground that effective leaders seemed to have:

- drive and energy;
- dedication;
- competitiveness;
- honesty;
- realism;
- maturity.

This list, however, gives no guidance as to the type of leader such qualities might produce; it could apply, for instance, to both Gandhi and Stalin. In business, it is more useful to look at the actions a leader has to take to be effective, rather than dwelling on vague qualities that may apply.

The secretarial team leader is employed to get the job done through the secretarial team. John Adair, in *Action Centered Leadership*, identified three areas needed for this to be achieved.

1. *The task.* The leader's job is to:
   - define the task;
   - construct a plan;
   - allocate work and resources;
   - control quality and pace of work;
   - check performance against the plan;
   - adjust the plan if necessary.
2. *The individual.* The leader's job is to:
   - attend to personal needs;
   - give praise and recognition;
   - exploit individual abilities;
   - train the individuals;
   - give individuals status.
3. *The team.* The leader's job is to:
   - set agreed standards;
   - maintain discipline;
   - build team spirit;
   - motivate and give recognition;
   - ensure good communications;
   - train the group.

This demonstrates that, for a team to be effective, the team needs team spirit and goals to aim at. The individual members of the team have ambitions and need to feel, and be, part of an active team. The team leader's job, irrespective of the level of management, is to facilitate the above. A breakdown or neglect in any one area will in due course affect the others, and prevent the job being done as effectively as it could be.

Leaders must have a strategy. Examination of a cross section of leaders has identified four elements:

1. Effective leaders paint a vivid and compelling vision of the results they want to achieve. This vision grabs the imagination of the team and gets its full attention.
2. Effective leaders forcefully communicate their vision in such simple and clear terms that it makes sense to the team and everyone becomes committed to it.
3. Effective leaders are dedicated to the vision, and their display of personal commitment to the course of action, encourages the team to trust the leader in its pursuit of the goals.
4. Effective leaders are able to use and manage their talents creatively. They know they have the capacity to build on their talents and have learned to compensate for their shortcomings. Often they can quickly see the requirements of the task, fit the skills to it, and then put all their energies into the task without any thought of it going wrong.

So the secretarial team leader must build the team, maintain the team, and look after the individuals within the team. Maintenance includes rebuilding the team with new entrants.

Effective team leaders must also:

- detach themselves from day-to-day detail and issues concerning systems and people;
- take on responsibility for goals, and demonstrate a personal positive attitude toward them;
- be good communicators, be open and honest and stir up strong positive emotions in team members;
- be proactive and create new ideas rather than reacting to other people's ideas;
- keep the team's vision and purpose clearly in mind, and focus team efforts to the achievement of the vision;
- deal with all team members in a consistent and evenhanded manner;
- be willing to accept new ideas and to learn, and regularly create new visible issues for debate within the team;
- openly demonstrate interest in team members and be aware of what effect decisions have upon them;
- encourage challenge and invite new solutions to old problems;
- judge ideas on the basis of merit, not on the basis of where they originated;
- be coach, motivator, and custodian of morale for the team;
- be a change agent, welcome change and act as a champion for change for the team;
- evaluate the team's performance openly and honestly and discuss the evaluation with the team;
- accept criticism of the team as a basis for improvement, not as a platform for defense;
- communicate positive and negative feedback as appropriate;
- not deny or excuse waste, inefficiency, or lost time;
- see the work of the team in relation to the larger organization;
- assign work to the team with regard to task needs and team capability rather than on the basis of personal bias.

Your style of leadership

So far we have considered the qualities of leadership and what leaders are meant to do; let us now consider your own leadership style. Leadership is about taking actions, and about dealing with people. If we put these together, we have the way you behave in your relationships with others. First, let us establish that there is no correct, or single, way of dealing with people. All your team members are different and all will respond best to different forms of approach in different situations. The critical test of a good leader is to the extent to which that person can apply the most suitable behavior to meet the needs of the individual and circumstances at any given time.

Tannenbaum and Schmidt developed a very useful model called "The spectrum of leadership styles" (see Figure 1). The model gives seven alternatives for the way that you, as leader, can get things done. Let us examine each of these in turn.

1. *Tell.* At the extreme left-hand side of the model, the authority exercised by the leader is at its maximum. The leader tells the team what to do; normally no discussion or challenge is invited or accepted. It is a very dictatorial style and probably—in the modern business environment—only appropriate in a crisis. If the building is collapsing it is sensible to adopt this style and tell your team to "Get out of here—now!"

2. *Sell.* Moving one stage to the right side is "sell." Here you communicate your decision, but give reasons for it, often stating the advantages to all of the decision. This is a useful approach when your hands are tied and you recognize that your team will have to implement the decision whether you like it or not.

3. *Explain.* Here, again, you have made your decision but—believing in your judgment—you are prepared to invite questions on your decision. This allows the members of your team to become clearer in their own minds as to the reasons and background for your decision.

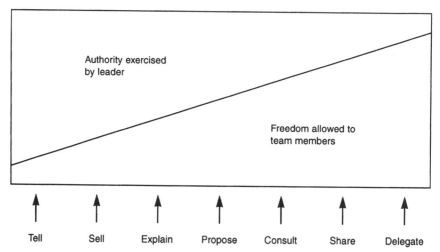

Figure 1 The spectrum of leadership styles.

4. *Propose.* The midpoint of the model is to propose your decision. By putting your decision in the form of a proposal, you are inviting debate. This signals that you are open to reviewing your thinking in the light of others' opinions before finalizing your decision.
5. *Consult.* Moving now to the right-hand side, consulting means getting suggestions from your team before making your decision. You will be adding your team's ideas to your own and then agreeing on any decision with the team.
6. *Share.* Giving even more authority and freedom to your team here, you define the limits within which decisions must be taken and ask the team to make the decision with or without you. Your job as team leader is to spell out the opportunities and the restrictions (e.g., budgets, resources, deadlines) that the decision must be made within.
7. *Delegate.* At the extreme right-hand side of the model, you delegate the decision and let the team decide within the limits you have set. Here you are giving almost complete freedom to your team. If you do decide to take part in the decision making process, it will be as a team member, not as a team leader.

Today's staff do not like being told what to do; they want to share in decisions. The more they are allowed to participate, the greater is their commitment to the decision. Leadership style is catching: your team will copy your style, because you are their team leader and they will think that is the way it ought to be done. Gradually your style becomes the "house style" of your department. Flexing your style from left to right across the model is not easy. The decision of what style to adopt is a mixture of your own preferred personal style, the needs of the situation and the needs of the team. The more you learn to flex your style the easier it will become, because you will have more reference points to choose from. Don't worry about making mistakes at first.

Situation leadership

Finally, let us look at situation leadership. Here, before making any decision or inviting discussion on a decision, the team leader should consider three aspects, which can be represented in a simple model (see Figure 2).

1. The leader. Here the team leader has to conduct a personal audit as follows:
   - Do I have sufficient experience to do the job?
   - Am I the best person to lead the team in this situation?
   - What training will I need?
   - What outside help may I need to bring in?
   - Have I got a clear enough vision of what is needed to be able to communicate it to the team?
   - What are the consequences of success and failure?
2. The team. The same audit process will follow but this time jointly with the team.
   - Do we have sufficient skills in the team to do the job?
   - What training may be necessary?
   - Do we need to bring in external help?

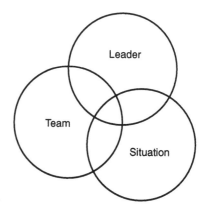

Figure 2 Situation leadership.

- Are we well motivated for this task?
- What will be the consequences of success and failure for the team?

3. The situation. Again the audit process is followed jointly with the team.
   - Do we know enough about the situation, and what extra information do we need?
   - Have we been in this situation before?
   - Is this a unique situation or can we recall similar situations to aid the learning process?
   - What will be the consequences of success or failure for the organization?
   - Can we look at other people's experiences in this situation?

You are invited to test your leadership style using the following questionnaire. Answer in the following way:

1. I rarely believe this or act in this manner.
2. I sometimes believe this or act in this way.
3. I often believe this or act in this way.
4. I strongly believe this and act accordingly as much as I can.

Questions

	1	2	3	4
1. I delegate as often as possible.	1	2	3	4
2. I socialize with my team.	1	2	3	4
3. I forgo personal preferences for the benefit of my team.	1	2	3	4
4. I share decesions with my team.	1	2	3	4
5. I show enthusiasm and commitment.	1	2	3	4
6. I practice openness with my team.	1	2	3	4
7. I seek recognition and reward on behalf of my team.	1	2	3	4
8. I encourage training for my team members.	1	2	3	4
9. I share setbacks with my team.	1	2	3	4
10. I explain my decisions to the team.	1	2	3	4

11. I use my skills and experience for the benefit of the
    team as opposed to my own personal gain.   1   2   3   4
12. I coach my team to win.   1   2   3   4
13. Without me, the team would not function as effectively
    as it does.   1   2   3   4
14. I enjoy consulting with my team.   1   2   3   4
15. I encourage challenge in the team.   1   2   3   4
16. I share success with my team.   1   2   3   4
17. I enjoy flexing my leadership style.   1   2   3   4
18. I exploit the talents of my team.   1   2   3   4

The maximum score is 72 and the minimum score 18.

A score of 18 to 36 indicates that although you are a team leader, you are not adopting a leadership style that will encourage a team to grow. You may be too dictatorial, often putting yourself before the team.

A score of 37 to 54 suggests that you are showing commitment to your team and involving them in decision making and development. Check your low scores, i.e., 1 or 2, and work through your thinking again.

A score of 55 to 72 demonstrates that as a team leader you flex your style, trust in your team, and are prepared to sacrifice short-term gain for long-term team building.

Understanding the Members of Your Team

Each member of the secretarial team brings to the team three distinct and valuable facets:

- individual skills;
- individual personality;
- individual preferred team role.

One of the team maintenance tasks carried out by the team leader is to create a balanced team. A balanced team makes the best use of skills, personalities, and roles. There is of course a relationship between all three. In particular, personality will often determine the role you prefer to play in teams.

Each team member has unique thoughts, motivations, expectancies, perceptions, values, and attitudes. But it is *behavior* that is the only part of an individual that we actually see. For that reason role behavior, or role playing, in the team is of the utmost importance because of the effect it has upon the other team members.

The combined behavior of all the team members, i.e., the ways in which they do their jobs and the ways in which they interact with each other, is called *group dynamics*. Some people consistently display the same behavior in all situations at work because they are sticking to preferred roles; usually their natural roles. Other team members may vary team roles depending on the situation.

One role to look out for is the personal role. Here, for whatever reason, the team member has decided to disregard the needs of the task or the team but plays a role for a personal motive. Typically such roles include: pretending to be very bright and motivated; pretending to be switched off; and pretending not to understand. Such people are described as having hidden agendas. A typical reason for a hidden agenda would be the hope that, if someone pretends not to know something, you will not give a particular job to that person.

Group dynamics is the balance between the needs of the task and the needs of the team. In group dynamics, the team leader's role is to build a winning team by:

- learning to identify the preferred and natural roles of the team members;
- encouraging team members to take on more than one role as and when the situation and the team need it;
- playing missing roles themselves if a role gap is identified;
- detecting personal roles, identifying the hidden agendas, and bringing individuals around to supportive and preferred roles.

In the mid-1980s, one of the authors was working on a North Sea drilling platform, and observing the shift drilling crews. Oil drillers are by nature "doers"; they work in united and highly competitive teams; their task is to drill and push as much pipe as possible into the sea bed and rock. When, as occasionally happened, the drill bit broke, they had to discontinue drilling, pull up the pipe, and replace the drill bit. This lost time caused frustration and loss of morale. At this point, the tool pusher (supervisor) would switch from his team leader role to a caring role, to comfort the team, override the disappointment, and rebuild morale so that the team could quickly become a winning unit again. The reason why the team leader had to take the caring role was that in a team of doers no one else had yet learned to play a caring role.

The following team roles have been identified by the authors during the past ten years or so while working for multinationals and some of the United Kingdom's largest companies in the United Kingdom, Europe, Africa, and the United States.

The beaver

No team can function without the beaver. Indeed, in a secretarial team of, say, six to ten people, you will normally find more than one beaver. As the name implies, the beaver is the worker, the person who enjoys getting the job done. That is why that individual was received into the role. The characteristics of the beaver are:

- needs to work in teams, and needs to feel safe in the team structure;
- team player and often puts the team before individual recognition;
- not overtly competitive, but enjoys the team winning;
- will confuse efficiency with effectiveness;
- very task-oriented, with little regard to people issues;

- not very responsive to change, especially where it impacts upon working methods;
- likes working within an ordered structure and gets worried if other team members break the rules.

The challenger

All successful teams need a challenger. In a time of fast-moving change, the challenger will challenge the accepted response, as well as what the organization is trying to achieve. An open challenger will question within and without the team. But if the organization—because of its culture—regards a challenger as a troublemaker, then the challenger may go underground and be regarded as a rebel. That person may adopt a negative role.

In a negative role, the challenger will be a blocker, or a nitpicker, but in a positive role will refocus the team, and question the team goals, inspiring new ideas. The characteristics of the challenger are:

- very inquisitive and curious mind;
- often a growing visionary, who is a follower, not a leader at this stage of personal development;
- can be cynical, but this cynicism is often a role play defensive mechanism to compensate for natural optimism;
- usually a generalist with a very broad-based education;
- enjoys the role, and seeks recognition from fellow team members more than company recognition;
- quick to learn, which is after all the basis of the challenge.

The coach

Teams can function very effectively without anyone in the coach role, but they miss certain qualities, including having fun. The coach seeks responsibility for the morale of the team, and adds the final polish to a motivated group. Many organizations, acknowledging the lack of experienced coaches in teams, have introduced coaching skills as part of management development training.

The coaching role is not necessarily a primary one, but more a chosen secondary team role. There is normally room for only one coach in a team. In smaller teams of, say, four to six people, the team leader will often take the coaching role. The characteristics of the coach are:

- has a reputation for getting the best out of people;
- often a hard taskmaster, who demands 110 percent effort;
- usually a retired successful type, with a great deal of experience, who no longer has anything to prove;
- a well-balanced and mature person who enjoys people skills;
- likes winning and sees his role as facilitating the win;
- flexible and can apply coaching skills to a great variety of teams.

The confessor

Teams need confessors at various points of team development, but in particular when going through a change process. Confessors are carers to whom members of the team will go with their troubles. It is often a difficult role to pinpoint at the outset of team development because of the natural secrecy of the role. The confessor is not a primary role; it is often a secondary role of one of the beavers.

Because the fast pace of change in our organizations can upset team members who are having to face new organization structures as well as new technologies, the role of the confessor in teams is becoming more important. It is not a role that the team leader can easily adopt. It is essential in the construction of a team that at least one person is chosen or encouraged to be the team confessor. The characteristics of the confessor are:

- a reputation for openness and honesty, and for dealing with people and situations evenly and fairly;
- often secretive by nature, attracting secrets from others;
- high interpersonal skills, enjoys dealing with people;
- can be manipulative and cause problems in the team if motives are wrong, but positive confessors are essential to the team maintenance needs, and will deflect organization strife;
- because of the role the individual adopts, can become highly stressed and may need additional support from the team leader;
- normally an outgoing person who can identify others with problems, because she has close interpersonal relationships with other team members.

The explorer

Teams do not necessarily need explorers, whose primary role is to obtain information and form relationships with other teams. The explorer is not a primary role and can be the secondary role of any team member. In our experience, explorers are often frustrated leaders, who accept that the leadership role is not to be theirs, yet need an active role to make a contribution to the team.

If your team is taking on new tasks, and new technology, then the explorer will be invaluable in collecting facts and opinions on how other teams coped with the new situations. Explorers build bridges between other teams, departments, and individuals, and thus by relating other people's views, can have a positive effect on the motivation of the team. In long-established teams that have become inert in function and social skills, the explorer is essential to refocus the team to the wider world outside. The relationships they form will also be very useful in identifying tasks and people necessary for the growth of the team. The characteristics of the explorer are:

- adventurous and curious, as the name suggests the explorer lives in a greater world and relates experiences with enthusiasm to the team;

- usually gregarious and friendly, seeking people contact and forming strong relationships;
- often a self-starter and achiever, using the team as a base camp to fulfill his preferred role;
- good communicator, with the ability to impart information honestly for the benefit of the team;
- unless restrained, may lead you into unflown skies as she seeks to push the boundaries of the team ever back;
- never gives up exploring, which is good for the synergy and development of the team

The librarian

This is not a primary role. The librarian fulfills a very useful secondary role in that all information about the team will be recorded by her. The role itself can change depending on the development and mastery of data base systems. With little or no recorded data the role is very important, and the importance will contract as data is recorded and stored. Certainly the explorer and team leader will draw upon the information and knowledge held by the librarian.

In teams that use complex data systems, the librarian will be the person who makes best use of the facilities, monitoring the data base for the benefit of the team. The characteristics of the librarian are:

- more interested in things than people, and therefore a loner;
- pays great attention to detail and can get lost in organization and structure;
- a quiet person with few verbal skills, who prefers to communicate through data systems;
- appears to be very hard working, but in reality is not very effective;
- living through data makes that person historical rather than visionary;
- a team player, very open to structured change.

The peacemaker

Teams can function without a peacemaker but sometimes decision making is slower. A sense of healthy argument and fun is diminished. The peacemaker is the person who pours oil on troubled waters and seeks the unification of the team after friction has occurred. The role is one that allows skilled teams to use management by conflict, i.e., allowing people to be open, honest, and vocal, and to put their views forcibly in meetings. The peacemaker is concerned with the maintenance of the team and sees the team as a whole rather than a collection of individuals.

A very strong and forceful peacemaker, however, may quash healthy and strong discussion too early, and should be directed by the team leader to hold fire until the dealer has had a chance to run. The characteristics of the peacemaker are:

- prefers dealing with people rather than things;
- very logical, patient, and good communicator;
- high assertion skills that are applied to beating the problem, not the team;
- often does not get involved in the content of debate but concentrates on the process;
- very objective and unemotional about problem solving;
- easily bored and will change strategy to get peace at all cost.

The pragmatist

The pragmatic role is becoming increasingly important in a pragmatic society. The pragmatist demonstrates to the team how to make the impossible possible, often taking the visionaries' ideas and converting them into a sensible and politically acceptable organizational plan. In a business world of fast change, it is the pragmatist's role to encourage the team to let go of old ideas, and look at new ways of doing things. Obviously a combination of the pragmatist and the challenger will provide a strong focus to move the team ahead.

Disillusioned pragmatists can be a nuisance to the team by being cynical and skeptical about new ideas, and need to be held in check by the team leader. Positive pragmatists do, however, refocus the team's efforts and get things achieved. The characteristics of the pragmatist are:

- a team player, putting the team before the problem;
- often a failed visionary, who has not yet found a mission in life;
- very realistic to the point of sounding negative;
- can be immature and have a childish style in meetings, and easily gets annoyed;
- often from a scientific or mathematical background;
- suspicious of people's motives, but a good ally when convinced;
- enjoys turning visions into bricks and mortar.

The referee

As the name suggests, the referee is the person who brings independent focus to the team. Often this secondary but necessary role will emerge when the team would seem at loggerheads with the organization itself. If the business is installing a new computer system and there is resistance from the secretarial team, then the referee—using information from the explorer and allowing the challenger to question—will act as a bridge between the team and the organization to steer the system through.

Because team members find it difficult to be totally independent, an outsider may be brought into the team to play this role. Management consultants often find themselves in this situation. Referees, although team players, need to be able to demonstrate an independence from the team culture; making sure that the team keeps within the rules of the organization but challenging in an empowering way. Characteristics of the referee are:

- will be a strong team player, with great commitment to the task and to people;
- will have strong influencing and negotiating skills, with a reputation for dealing with people on a level playing field;
- a natural role player who can flex his style to exploit the best in any situation;
- neutrality based on self-confidence and the need to facilitate a team win;
- independent minded, with the optimism and courage to seek fair play;
- logical and decisive mind.

The visionary

Teams without a visionary become bored and tired. The visionary is a primary role, whose job is to look beyond the day-to-day team tasks and seek the larger picture of what the team should be doing, and could be doing. The visionary is instrumental in allowing the team to take on more responsibility and more exciting tasks. Unchecked visionaries can lead teams into trouble by leading them into areas that are of no concern of the team, or that they do not have the skill base to do. The visionary often acts alone until she is sure of her vision, which she then, crusader-like, expects the team to follow. In modern team building, we often see the team leader acting as the visionary for the team. Characteristics of the visionary are:

- impatience, with a tendency to expect everyone to follow the vision, however badly it is explained;
- very optimistic, seeing problems as opportunities;
- very open and honest, with a freewheeling sense of disclosure that can be misunderstood;
- living in the big picture, she is bored by and ignores detail;
- a thinker rather than a doer, who does not get a lot done but contributes greatly to the synergy of the team;
- allies herself with anyone who supports "the vision."

Balanced and nonbalanced teams

Having looked at the team roles in some detail, we can consider balanced and nonbalanced teams. In the past, very few organizations found it necessary to form teams, let alone balance them. But increasingly companies are acknowledging the benefits of teamwork in bringing together task skill and personalities, to get the best job done. These days, with team building being recognized as a management tool, a lot of effort is being put into achieving the right combinations of people. In some of the organizations we are working for, the teams themselves are now having their say as to team replacements, concentrating on the role and personality as well as the skill base.

Obviously a balanced team will depend on the function of the team. A balanced secretarial team should consist of skilled secretarial staff, i.e., beavers, as well as a leader, a visionary to explore what the team could contribute to the organization, and a challenger to focus on new working methods and new technology. In the absence of a visionary, the leader may well assume that role as well. If we are considering a typing pool, it might be sufficient to have only a leader and a number of beavers. In our view, however, a well-balanced secretarial team, servicing a modern charge or organization, should have a team balanced as follows:

Primary role	*Secondary role*
Leader	Coach
Visionary	Explorer
Challenger	Pragmatist
Beaver	Confessor
Beaver	Peacemaker
Beaver	Librarian
Referee	Optional

This is a recommended list of primary and secondary roles, and these are of course interchangeable. Obviously the smaller the team the more primary and secondary roles need to be picked up by each individual. In larger teams of, say, eight to ten people, team members will have more chance to gravitate toward preferred roles that they feel more comfortable in.

Secretarial team leaders who now wish to identify the tasks and roles of team members should compile a team inventory sheet for all team members as follows.

Name

Job description

Specific skills

1.

2.

3.

Preferred primary role

Actual primary role

Preferred secondary role

Observed secondary roles:

1.

2.

3.

This team roles audit is the first stage of balancing your team. Don't forget to include yourself.

Stress and Your Team

An important task of the secretarial team leader is to manage stress by monitoring it in the team, recognizing potential sources of stress, and removing those sources for individual team members. This person must also be able to give advice when and where necessary, recommending expert help when needed.

At its simplest, stress is caused as a result of the interaction between the demands of the situation and the individual's ability to meet those demands.

In early times, the response to stress was fright, fight, or flight. To enable people to deal with danger, the senses became more acute, the heart rate increased, hair stood on end, and so on. Modern people, particularly in corporate environments, get into the habit of putting the lid on these instinctive reactions, which results in pent-up feelings and the occasional boil over.

Stress results from the way an individual perceives the situation, and this has its foundations in experience, training, and abilities. Therefore, the world around us produces potential stressors (i.e., those things that can cause us stress) and it is only the judgment made by the individual that her environment is threatening in some way that produces stress. For instance, in recognizing that things may be potentially stressful for you, imagine that:

- you are a blind person shopping in a busy street;
- you are a deaf person taking part in a potentially explosive demonstration;
- you have just inherited $3 million.

Each of the above will create potential stressors for people who are not used to such situations.

Your work becomes stressful when challenging work goes beyond normal pressures to the point where you can't cope. When challenge ceases to be stimulating, when work becomes threatening, and when there always seems to be another pressure looming, you are beginning to suffer stress. Eventually you are unable to keep rising to the occasion; your performance starts to suffer.

Common causes of stress at work

Let us consider some of the more common causes of stress at work.

Increased and unwelcome responsibility

Many people are very happy doing the job they enjoy and were trained to do. Reorganizations and the need for more productivity often result in people working for more bosses than before, and some of those bosses are at a higher level in the organization.

Bad delegation

Many of our first- and second-line managers have never been trained in the art of delegation. This results in half-baked instructions, mistakes, and frustration. Delegation is outlined in the time management section of this book, beginning page 49.

Too close supervision and not being allowed to get on with the job

Some bosses are not very good at delegating work, and oversupervise others. This trend is increasing as companies are forced into more paper-bound checking routines brought about by legislation and initiatives such as total quality management.

Unreasonable and uneven workloads

Human nature dictates that work gravitates to the more able and better disposed secretaries. This can lead to intra- and inter-team conflict as well as stress.

New technology and working procedures

The pace of change in business is increasing, especially with work reengineering and information technology. This can put learning overload on many secretaries. Just as they learn to master a new system, e.g., Windows, a new one comes around the corner.

Fear of losing one's job and general insecurity

Constant reorganizations, benchmarking, reengineering, and announced global redundancies mean that many secretaries feel that their jobs are under threat, affecting their long-term view of their employment. They find themselves living and planning in the short term.

Poor relationships with the boss and the team

Some secretaries find themselves in declining relationships, often caused by the upheavals mentioned above, such as moving from one boss to another.

Under- and over-promotion, and the sense of feeling trapped

Because of the oftentimes mentioned fast changes, many secretaries find themselves doing jobs that years ago a junior would have done, whereas others are promoted beyond their level of competency. Yet others are trapped, going nowhere, with ambitions that will not be satisfied.

Lack of management support

Without realizing it, management often gives the wrong level of support to secretarial teams. Problems arise in general communications, uncertainty about what is happening around the company, and restricted freedom of action.

The inner self

Another very important cause of stress at work is the inner self. Individuals often fail to understand their own needs, motives, or desires. You or members of your team may lack flexibility to cope with change. Some individuals are nervous about moving out of their current area of training and expertise. Many people have unrealistic expectations about themselves and others.

Women and men share the above difficulties. However, there are certain potential stressors that are specific to each sex in our current society. As the majority of secretaries at the present time are women, it is valuable to examine the extra pressures that women in work have to cope with.

1. *Work versus home.* Despite the emergence of the "new man," the majority of household situations conform to a historical norm; in these cases it is women who have to cope with working and running a home. This is all the more intense when there are the added pressures of bringing up children. Further pressures are added in times of recession and redundancy, when circumstances can leave women as the sole earner in households where men are ill-equipped to deal with role changes.
2. *Smaller peer group and role models.* Because fewer women are given managerial responsibility, there are fewer colleagues to discuss issues with and fewer role models to learn with and from.
3. *Harassment.* Women, generally speaking more than men, are subject to sexual harassment. They suffer accusations of being feminist or aggressive when they defend their positions, often in situations where men would be applauded for the same responses. Women are still regarded by some male colleagues as the gentle sex, and not expected to get angry in the same ways.
4. *Experimental women.* In too many of our organizations, women are being used as tokens, promoted unreasonably so that the company can point to its policy of equal opportunities. At the same time, other women may be denied promotion they are rightly due. Pressure is added when the accusation is made that individuals have been promoted because they are women. Whether or not that happens to be true, it is not the individual's fault. We have not yet grown out of the traditional work partitioning of women in our organizations.

Effects of stress

Having looked at some of the most common causes of stress, let us now examine the results: the effects of stress upon the individual. Reactions to stress can be mental, behavioral, and physical. The secretarial team leader should be on the lookout for these effects in team members. All stress factors have a tendency to damage the individual's effectiveness at work. In general, stress makes you preoccupied, introspective, emotional, and unhappy. It saps your confidence and hinders your concentration.

Mental stress signs

These normally show themselves as an irrational feeling of anxiety, a sense of panic, of not wanting to be here. There is a general feeling that life and work is not fun any more, and a general lack of sensitivity to other people. These particular warning signals are difficult to read at first, but should stress continue, they tend to manifest themselves in behavioral and physical signals that are much easier to read.

Behavioral stress signs

These include the following:

■ withdrawal from others, not wanting to be sociable or to discuss problems, not taking part in recreational activities;

- inability to make decisions or prioritize work, often coupled with making mistakes even in routine tasks;
- forgetting things and arriving at meetings and appointments poorly prepared;
- staying late at work and taking work home;
- not taking vacations;
- late arrival at work and casual absenteeism.

Physical stress signs

These include the following:

- drinking heavily, taking drugs;
- taking less trouble over appearances;
- rapid weight loss or gain;
- headaches, indigestion, overtiredness, skin irritation, and breathlessness;
- poor posture, cramps, sweating, clammy feeling, and low vitality.

The secretarial team leader must be on the alert for these and similar signs. If you are aware that you or any member of your team are displaying a large or increasing number of the above, then you should seek help without delay.

The following questionnaire provides a self-analysis.

	Very rarely true				Usually true	
1. I plan my lifestyle to be healthy.	1	2	3	4	5	6
2. I know how to switch off and relax.	1	2	3	4	5	6
3. I plan for time off and take it.	1	2	3	4	5	6
4. I do not take on more than I can deal with.	1	2	3	4	5	6
5. I get enough sleep.	1	2	3	4	5	6
6. My personal life is in control.	1	2	3	4	5	6
7. I organize my work into urgent and nonurgent.	1	2	3	4	5	6
8. I don't let things get me down.	1	2	3	4	5	6
9. I am confident in what I do.	1	2	3	4	5	6
10. I am very rarely off from work.	1	2	3	4	5	6
11. I achieve what I want to do.	1	2	3	4	5	6
12. I get along well with my colleagues.	1	2	3	4	5	6
13. I look forward to going to work.	1	2	3	4	5	6
14. I have no trouble concentrating on issues.	1	2	3	4	5	6
15. I am happy with my position in the organization.	1	2	3	4	5	6
16. I enjoy my life outside of work.	1	2	3	4	5	6
17. I recover from bad moods quickly.	1	2	3	4	5	6

Score

75–102: You are well balanced and very good at handling stress.

49–74: Some pressures are making you stressful. Go over the questions where you have scored 3 or less and discuss the result with a close colleague or friend.

48 and below: You probably need help with some of the issues that are causing you stress. Look at each low score question and decide why your score is so low, and make a specific action plan of what you intend to do about it.

Challenge versus stress

The secretarial team leader should at all times understand the difference between challenging work and stressful work.

Challenging work is what people want. They are trained and rewarded for doing it. It motivates people and gives them a sense of achievement and self-esteem. Stressful work is what people sometimes have to cope with. Often they are not trained to deal with it and even extra reward does not compensate for the damage it can do in loss of self-esteem and demotivation. Frustration leads to mental and physical health problems.

No two people are the same, so stress has to be dealt with on an individual basis. Take expert advice as often as needed. Stress is now recognized as a huge waste of money in industry and commerce. Sickness alone caused by occupational stress costs British industry about $4 billion each year. Stress leads to:

- high absenteeism;
- lawsuits and litigation;
- increased burnout of staff;
- increased accidents at work;
- decreased performance;
- high staff turnover;
- poor decision making.

Stress is what individuals experience when they decide that it is no longer possible to cope with the work demands. The secretarial team leader's job is to anticipate where stress can arise, communicate with the team collectively and individually, and counteract it.

Managing stress

People vary a great deal in how they cope with stress, and their ability to handle stress changes throughout life.

Often your ability to handle stress is linked to anchor points in your life. Anchor points are those blocks of stability that you turn to when all else is going wrong. Every individual has a collection of anchor points, but sometimes we do not recognize them as such, or recognize them too late. Some people lose them and live to regret it, although in time some of them can be replaced. But when these zones of stability are not available or lose their impact at the same time that stress occurs, people can get into serious trouble, including severe depression. Obviously if things go wrong at work and home at the same time, then the reliance on anchor points will be all the greater.

Examples of anchor points are:

- work—challenging and satisfying;
- home—partner, children, do-it-yourself;
- gardening—building, growing, tending;
- music—active and passive;
- friendship—social contact, close contact;
- recreation—reading, walking, movies;
- sport—competitive, team games, solo games;
- hobbies—collecting things, photography;
- art—painting, sculpture, passive and active.

Once you have established the source of stress, you can do something about it. Basically there are two ways of dealing with stress: the active and the passive. The active route is to meet the source of stress head on, get to the cause of the problem, and develop a personal action plan to deal with it. This will often entail talking it over with the person or people who, you feel, are causing the stress. The passive route is to avoid the cause of stress or attempt to deal with the symptoms without curing the problem.

Managing stress by the acceptance of who you are is about recognizing and accepting that on certain issues and in some circumstances:

- it is impossible for you to do everything;
- you have trouble listening to your feelings;
- you lack confidence;
- you are a perfectionist;
- you are an optimist;
- you feel you never have enough time to make decisions;
- you feel you should consult everyone before making important decisions;
- you are and can be overextended;
- you do get depressed;
- you do not like saying no to people.

How to increase your ability to cope with stress:

- Learn time management skills, so that you can plan and be better organized, and can prioritize your work.
- Plan your personal and work goals and understand the conflict that may arise between them.
- Plan vacation time, take short breaks, and make vacations a reward, not a chore.
- Make time for leisure, and make leisure a habit.

- Do the things that require your maximum concentration when you are at your best.
- Do not postpone important matters that are unpleasant, because they will only play on your mind.
- Take care of your health, take regular exercise; cut down on bad habits, such as a bad diet.
- Encourage openness and communication in yourself and people around you.
- Get trained to take control of your personal development.
- Understand that stress is just another work or personal problem.
- Take control of your own life (see Assertiveness in Volume 1, Part 4 of *The Professional Secretary*).
- Learn how to get out of depression quickly.
- Learn how to let go.
- Enjoy being in a new situation.
- Don't get into the stress habit.
- Above all, learn to be happy with yourself the way you are.

When we first started training stress management, we issued guidelines in our work packs that outlined ways to reduce stress. Over time, we found that people remembered the rules more if they were issued with humor, in the negative. The following is therefore a what-not-to-do list.

The APW Training 12-point plan for creating maximum stress at work

For secretarial team leaders:
1. Only communicate to your boss; never consult your team.
2. Always ask someone else to communicate bad news; better still, order him to.
3. If you must communicate, do it by letter or memo, never verbally.
4. Discourage open debate by belittling the questioner.
5. Always use politics or secret rules as an excuse for not being open.
6. Ridicule any new ideas from your team and treat them with suspicion.
7. Criticize freely and withhold recognition and praise.
8. Regard all problems as failure; discourage people from drawing problems to your attention.
9. Make full use of restrictions or hierarchical passwords in your data base systems.
10. Regard open communication by management down the line as a dismissive offense.
11. In meetings, always encourage point-scoring and in-fighting; praise the winner.
12. Restate the company rules as often as possible.

Understanding, Learning, and Training

I hear and I forget,

I see and I remember

I do and I understand (old Chinese saying).

In order to train, and to recognize the best training provisions, it is necessary to understand how people learn, and therefore how to adapt your teaching and training to meet the varied needs of your team. In some large organizations, you may have the availability of a professional training department, but in our experience, most training sections have turned themselves into training administrators and only identify suitable training courses, or bring in outside trainers. In smaller organizations, the secretarial team leader will have no choice but to take on the training role in any case. Your job is therefore not only on-the-job training but also the identification of training needs and courses that will suit both the individual and the team.

One of the problems of understanding learning is that everyone has been to school and many people go on to some form of training or further education. This unfortunately leads some people to think that they are experts in training and learning. Only recently we were told by a production manager of a chemical plant in the North East of England that he could provide trainers from his staff with no difficulty, even though the people he was thinking of were trained in neither training nor teaching methods.

One of the first principles of learning is to consider how adults like to learn. In general, people in this country have been taught by rote, e.g., learning the multiplication tables by heart, and if people have learned in that way, they will feel comfortable in that style. But there is more than rote learning, so let us look at the styles of adult learning.

The idealistic learner

Characteristics:
- the builder, the thinker, the reasoner;
- likes to discover things for herself;
- self-paced, allowing time for discovery;
- uses deductive reasoning, from general principles to specific conclusions.

Dislikes:
- being told what to do;
- too much structure, too many rules;
- having to work through step-by-step detail.

Preferred learning style:
- sharing opinions, values, ideas;

- group discussion;
- self-appraisal and self-evaluation;
- goal setting;
- participative management;
- problem solving.

The pragmatic learner

Characteristics:
- "I'll believe it when I see it";
- skills training are learned only when on the job;
- relevant learning takes place only when it occurs in the environment where it is to be applied;
- you learn in the "real world," through life experience.

Dislikes:
- residential training;
- classroom settings;
- abstract theories.

Preferred learning style:
- custom-designed training for their unique work situation;
- individual coaching;
- demonstration and practice;
- job-related exercises.

The realistic learner

Characteristics:
- good at time management;
- very highly motivated in doing what he is trained to do;
- works at a fast pace;
- prefers structure and facts.

Dislikes:
- dealing with people;
- team building activities;
- theory, abstract concepts;
- group problem solving;
- discovery experiences.

Preferred learning style:
- structured, programmed instruction that has explicit outcomes and clear goals;
- how-to workshops;
- computer-based training;
- programs based on hard, fast data;

- working through systems, procedure-oriented material;
- clearly defined cause-and-effect relationships.

The existentialistic learner

Characteristics:
- no one way is the right way to do something;
- likes to prove herself;
- high regard for her own and others' peculiar strengths and abilities;
- believes there are many effective ways to produce the same results;
- deals with situations and contingencies;
- uses deductive reasoning from particular facts to general conclusions.

Dislikes:
- set procedures;
- the one right way approach;
- lack of flexibility;
- lack of choice.

Preferred learning style:
- working with other people;
- team building;
- programs that show understanding, sensitivity, and respect for others' way of doing things;
- clearly defined objectives;
- freedom to design their own strategies for accomplishing those objectives.

Summary

The secretarial team leader should look at the team and recognize the preferred learning styles of team members. People go through learning cycles and may change from one to another. A snapshot picture is as follows.

- Team members who recognize the value of other people's experience and have a strong sense of values and reasons for doing things are *idealists*.
- Team members who know how complex the world is, realize the organization is too valuable to experiment with and live in the real world are *pragmatists*.
- Team members who take pleasure from action, like doing things and have concluded that most work requires effort and courage are *realists*.
- Team members who recognize a logical and understandable world, recognize the value of people and consider weaknesses as well as strengths are *existentialists*.

When you have established the preferred learning style of your team members, the next step is to look at why some people are happy to remain in skill-based tasks and jobs, whereas others will seek higher-level work and, often, promotion. Factors influencing this are complex as they are based on individual upbringing, type of education, past experiences, past successes and failure, social contact, and self-esteem. However, for simplicity we can look at the characteristics of the two types of people.

Skill-based people will often demonstrate the following characteristics at work:
- great pride in their work;
- enjoy doing things;
- prefer structure, routine, and repetitive work;
- resistant to change;
- lack work initiative;
- want to be experts;
- prefer to be closely supervised;
- role play humility—"I'm only the secretary";
- do not realize their full potential;
- live in short-term work perspectives;
- seek job security;
- work to live.

Higher-level work people will often demonstrate the following characteristics at work:
- ambitious—driven to seek full potential;
- easily bored with routine tasks;
- enjoy problem solving and decision making;
- learn from others;
- seek strategic roles;
- seek empowerment and recognition;
- role play many alternative roles;
- welcome change;
- challenge the accepted;
- willing to take risks;
- want to increase their repertoire of skills and behavior;
- live to work.

Other factors influencing people's ability to learn and develop are of a more general nature, such as morale, motivation, maturity of the individual, time pressures, and mental speed. We can now consider these in the training context. Training can be split into two main areas:

- *skills training,* designed to increase people's immediate effectiveness, by improving their natural and clerical skills;
- *development training,* designed to improve people's overall long-term effectiveness by improving their higher-level skills and changing their attitudes toward the organization and work.

Therefore, we train people to obtain and retain a competitive edge. Part of this competition lies in new technology, new working methods, changing organizational structures, and dealing with people in a new way, i.e., empowerment based on the idea that for "every pair of hands you get a free brain." Only by improving people's skills, knowledge, and attitudes so that they can change their way of doing things can we get the best out of our people.

Morale and motivation are therefore very important. In an insecure job market, individuals must remember that new and transferable skills are the secret to employment survival. But people will only truly be motivated to learn if they have a problem to solve, and do not just learn the solution but become part of the solution making process. Your role as secretarial team leader is to create a working environment where your team feels safe to question their attitudes, recognize their own problems, and solve problems in cooperation with you and other colleagues.

The factors influencing maturity in learning change during the development of the individual and depend upon circumstances. The team leader will have to consider on an individual basis the level of maturity people are at and why. How stable is the individual? What is his emotional and psychological state? How realistic and flexible is the individual? What level of emotional support and security does the individual need? For example, a young person getting married, taking out a mortgage, and discovering his job is under threat will welcome and seek new skills training; a person at age 63, two years away from retirement with a good pension, will be less motivated. However, our young person getting married may have decided on his career and might not be so enthused about development training as, say, a 35-year-old secretary who wishes to advance her career. Obviously the circumstances of the individual might also change: even the person most open to development training may have a little trouble concentrating on his career track if he has just won or inherited $1 million!

Time pressures can also upset people's readiness to learn. If you are very busy, dealing with a backlog, and you are not really keeping up with the workload to your satisfaction, the last thing you may want to do is go to training courses. (How many times have we heard people say they haven't got the time to go to time management courses!) As trainers, we find it even worse when delegates say, at the beginning of the course, "Thank God I'm here, I needed a rest." Learning can only be executed when someone's mind is ready to accept new ideas and concepts. Plan your training when the team's or individual's workloads are least; otherwise they will be thinking of their immediate work, whereas in reality what they should be doing is being trained.

Mental speed is a difficult subject. Some people are quicker than others in mental agility. Mental speed is about alertness: how you feel that day, how you are motivated, the level of interest. Your memory plays a part: how quickly can you recall things? This may be dependent on how often you have had to do it. Mental speed involves conceptualization: painting a picture of what the solution may look like. People can be resistant to training and learning if they feel that their mental speed is not as fast as other team members' or colleagues.' The job of the team leader here is to avoid embarrassing a team member, by knowing whom not to pick on in the training situation, and whom to allow to work at her own speed. Training, like learning, is not a race with winners. At this level, all team members should enter the race and pass the finishing post at their own speed.

Preparing to teach

We must look at the preparation the secretarial team leader will need to do before running formal training sessions. As mentioned before, you can consult with training professionals at this point. It is useful to prepare a training preparation plan, as follows.

1. Establish with the team or the individuals what they need to learn, and evaluate what they already know. Distinguish between what is really necessary and what is useful revision.
2. Agree on what you need to teach, and what preparation is necessary, e.g., transcribing notes, getting handouts processed, what audiovisual aids are available.
3. Depending on their preferred learning styles, decide on the best teaching method to use. For:
   - *skills teaching*, use lectures, demonstrations, tutor groups, working at their own speed using interactive video or computer-based training;
   - *development training*, use lectures, role play exercises, tutor-led group discussion, structured modular learning, computer-assisted learning, and independent study, such as distance learning.
   - *attitudinal training*, use case studies, role play exercises, student-led tutorials, group discussion, off-site visits.
4. Depending on their motivation and maturity, you will need to agree on what degree of supervision your students will need. For individuals or groups that need a high degree of supervision, you will need to use tutor-led activities, i.e., lectures, or tutorials, whereas for student-centered learning you can combine tutorials with student-led case studies, games, and computer-based independent study.
5. You must consider the students and their attitudes to the learning process. Ask the following questions of yourself. Are the students motivated to learn? Are their minds open or closed? How well did they handle the previous learning sessions?

Adults have a lot of experiences to draw from and some will have learned from them. Adult learning is a move from dependence to independence, and most adults will want to learn if they can see the relevance and value of what they are learning and apply it to agreed goals. Adults are motivated to learn when they can relate what they are learning to past experiences.

In Kolb's model of learning (Figure 3), we can see that from a concrete experience learning progresses to the observation and reflection stage. Some people do not progress at this point, but form stereotypes and generalizations. These people are usually bigoted, live in restricted cultures, and are either very busy or too busy. For those who progress, after the reflection stage the individual will form abstract concepts, lessons, and then generalizations, so that these can be tested to renew the concrete experiences. Academic people often find this last stage a problem, and prefer to keep forming and reforming concepts, and lessons rather than to test the implications of the concepts, i.e., they will read and reread the manual but will not switch on the computer.

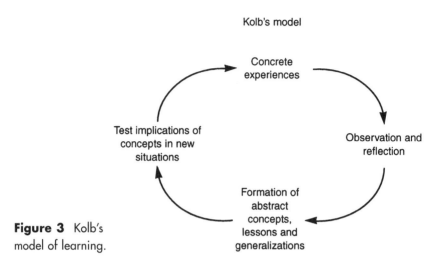

Figure 3 Kolb's model of learning.

Encouraging learning

Your job as the secretarial team leader is to create a learning atmosphere of openness and confidentiality, to make sure people are aware of their problems by asking questions, and to make people appreciate different interpretations of situations. Encourage people to think around the subject and explore ideas. Get your people actively involved in the learning process by getting them to do things to make the concepts concrete in their minds. Above all, remember that learning should be fun.

Interviewing

Secretarial teams, like all other teams, have to recruit new personnel at various times. It is important that the right person is selected so that the job is done with the maximum efficiency and the team and those affected by the team can work in harmony. It may be that the secretary is being recruited for part of a large secretarial pool, for a small department, as the only secretary to staff in the department or as the principal secretary to a senior manager or executive. Whatever the vacancy, the right person must be selected and the interview is a vital part of that selection process.

Secretaries already working in the company, along with other people in the department, should have a say in that selection process, particularly if team harmonics are to be balanced.

The interview arises out of a need for a particular member of staff. Before looking at interviewing techniques, we should briefly examine the situation that gives rise to the interview.

Where did the job come from?

Before the right person can be selected, the job she is being selected for must be properly understood. The first stage in the recruitment process is therefore to examine where the job came from.

If it is a new department, or a new secretarial appointment, there will be no history to examine. The parameters of the job have to be set by those for whom the secretary will be working, but they would do well to talk to other secretaries in the company and other departments, and possibly to have at least one of those on the interviewing panel. That could be you, and you will need to consider the interviewing skills outlined later in this section very carefully.

The job may arise because the previous occupant has left. Where possible, those doing the interviewing, and that job could also fall to you, should get as much information as possible about the job from the person leaving it. If she is leaving because of a promotion, she is very likely to be happy to discuss the job and its requirements with you. However, if she is leaving because she is dissatisfied with the job, she might have little interest in helping you or the company. However, it is important to try to have a termination interview and discover whether there are aspects of the job that are giving dissatisfaction and that could be corrected. This might make the job more acceptable to new candidates. (Of course, the process of appraisal and in-job interviews should have identified these problems with the previous employee; in this instance we must assume it has not.)

Finally, the job may have arisen because of ill health on the part of the previous holder, making a termination interview impractical. However, the message is clear: before you set out to fill a vacancy, as much as possible about that job should be known by those who are going to be doing the interviewing.

What is the job?

Before they interview candidates, all interviewers should have a job description that they can study. The job description should cover the following:

- job title;
- the department the job is in;
- details of the department, including number of staff, work volume;
- who the employee is responsible to;
- who is responsible to the employee;
- whether the employee is responsible for allocation of resources;
- terms and conditions of the job, including rates of pay, expected hours, any shifts, and flextime;
- future career prospects for the employee.

In creating a job description, it is often worth asking several different people in the department, and the previous occupant of the job, to prepare outline job descriptions for the same job. The differences are sometimes quite surprising!

What employee?

The people who have prepared the job descriptions should also be asked to fill out an employee description, setting out the characteristics that they believe will be held by the right candidate. Specifically, this broad description should include the following.

Physical requirements

Does the job have specific physical needs, e.g., is it one that demands great strength? Care must be taken not to create artificial criteria that are not dependent on the job itself and that might infringe on race relations legislation or equal opportunities legislation. Also consider the possibility of employing disabled people; unless the job cannot be done by someone who is physically or mentally challenged, make sure that the job is made available across the board.

Education and qualifications

Does the job require particular levels of education, degrees, or other specific qualifications?

Experience

Does the job require particular experience in, say, certain word processing programs, or certain filing experiences. For more senior secretaries, does the job require a background with more senior personnel, levels of confidentiality, and so on.

Personality

What sort of person would fit the job and the environment in which it takes place? Consider the personalities of the people already working in that area and make sure that the new candidate is at least going to complement that group.

Curriculum vitaes (CVs) often ask questions relating to sports enjoyed by particular people; companies are not necessarily interested in the sports for their own sake but for the attitude of the person that they reveal. If you are looking, for example, for a team member of a lively and interactive team, then you might consider someone who puts on her CV that she is interested in team sports and you might consider inappropriate someone who puts on his CV, "Only hobby is computer games in a dark locked room."

Special circumstances

Does the job involve, for example, a lot of overseas travel, which might not be convenient to a working mother or someone whose spouse worked peculiar shifts. Is a car essential? And so on.

Application forms

The company should devise an appropriate application form that enables the people selecting candidates to eliminate at the earliest possible stage those who are completely unsuitable. However, this is unlikely to be within the responsibilities of the secretary and is more likely to be dealt with by the human resources department; therefore, we will not cover that in this section. It is the awareness of the background and the interviewing techniques of the secretary likely to be involved in a selection interview that we are concerned with.

The interview

There might come a time when you have to sit on a selection interview panel, particularly if you will be working with the successful candidate. It is important that you should understand the purpose of the interview, how to prepare for the interview, rules for effective interviewing, and the conduct of the interview.

Purpose of the interview

The principal reasons for the interview are as follows.

To determine the candidate's motivation and behavior

You want to know why the candidate wants the job (because she "always wanted to do that job" or because "nothing better has come along for a while").

To determine the candidate's personality

In the interview, you should be able to discover how outgoing or reserved the candidate is, and to assess whether or not you feel she will complement the team and the environment she will be working in.

To confirm the factual information given by the candidate on the application form and her CV

The candidate will have made statements about her educational qualifications and experience. In the interview, you will want to make sure that she has given accurate information. You will want to examine, for example, the depth of the experience she claims; for example, she might say that she has had experience with a particular software program, but is that experience one hour or five years?

To give the candidate information about the job and the company and to allow her the opportunity of assessing whether or not the job is suitable

Interviewers often forget that the interview should be a two-way process for it to be effective. The candidate should be encouraged to ask questions about the job so that she can assess whether it is suitable for her. Interviewers who fail to recognize this tend to adopt an attitude that by employing someone they are doing her a favor. Almost certainly, such wrongheaded people will end up employing the wrong person.

Preparing for the interview

The interviewee is not the only one who has to prepare for the interview. If your first preparation for the interview is in front of the candidate, because you have not thought through the requirements of the interview or devised a plan of action for yourself, then you will not interview well. There are a number of main areas to consider.

Make sure that you have an up-to-date job description on hand

Not only should you have the job description, you should also have examined it thoroughly so that you do not have to keep referring to it during the interview. Remember that the candidate will be given the opportunity of questioning the panel about the job and you should be able to discuss it with the candidate fluently, with a sound basis of knowledge. You should, of course, also have the job description in your mind when assessing the candidate, as you should be matching ability or skill to requirement.

Digest written information about the candidate

Just as you should have thoroughly learned the job description, so you should have learned as much background information about the candidate as was available, by reading and digesting the information on her CV and application form.

List the key questions that you will ask

Interviewing should not be rigid and to a fixed formula. It should give room for a flexible response from both parties to the interview as it develops. However, it should be contained within a structure and that structure will be determined by key questions designed to assess the suitability of the candidate for the job in certain main areas. Those key questions should be on a notepad in front of you, to which you can glance during the interview and against which you can make summary notes (but see below). By having the key questions written down, you will make sure that you are not sidetracked by other members of the interviewing panel or the candidate and that the main questions are covered.

Make sure that the interview will not be interrupted by visitors or telephone calls

Emergencies or crises aside, the interview should not be interrupted. The candidate is naturally under some stress and interruptions would increase that stress unfairly and unreasonably. Furthermore, the interview will be of limited duration and there should be a focus of attention on the job at hand.

The office layout should be open and not restrictive

We refer nowadays to office body language: the way rooms are laid out reflects the personalities and attitudes of the people working in them. To reduce unnecessary and inappropriate stress at interviews, we would recommend that there is not a large dominating desk cutting off the interviewers from the candidate, but rather that the interview be conducted in as informal an environment as possible (a round table, comfortable chairs, and so on). If you are forced to interview at a desk, do not interview across it but rather sit diagonally across the corner, near each other. Provide appropriate refreshments. Consider arranging the interview room so that the candidate is facing the door. Remember that the candidate is in an unfamiliar environment and it is comforting for the candidate to have the psychological certainty that no one is silently entering the room or moving about in the room behind her (it could be argued that such psychological concerns hark back to our cave dwelling days, but whatever the reasons, it is a small gesture that creates a great deal of comfort).

Rules for effective interviewing

You want to get the best out of the interview and the best out of the candidate; you also want to present a good image of yourself and your company. Effective interviewing allows for this.

Those conducting the interview should not be rigid or authoritarian

Interviewers should ignore their own extreme views and prejudices; they should remember that they are assessing the candidate, not projecting themselves. Interviewers should be sensitive to the needs of the candidate, bearing in mind the stress that the candidate is under.

Interviewers should be trained in interviewing

It may be obvious that interviewing is no less a skill than any other and should be appropriately trained, with experience gained where possible. There are many organizations that can provide such training. The company should bear in mind that when engaging an employee it may be making an investment of many hundreds of thousands of dollars, and the candidate may be responsible for significantly increasing productivity or morale or, if badly chosen, significantly decreasing either. Despite this, many people employ interviewing techniques that are more amateurish and less reliable than the selection processes they would go through to choose a particular washing detergent in a supermarket.

Interviewers should not seek to create stress

The interview is an unusual situation, with an unnatural dynamic that will never arise again in that job. Even with a number of job changes, being interviewed is something very few people can claim to become expert at. Therefore, the interview is a naturally stressful situation. The interviewer should seek to reduce stresses, not increase them.

Some companies have policies of creating stress in order to test the candidate's ability to deal with pressure. In our experience, the unnaturalness of the situation ends up providing very little valuable information. Such pressure interviews were popular in the 1970s but have few modern advocates, as companies have realized the value of open and empowering work environments.

We recall being told of one technique in interviews of potential bus conductors and drivers. The interviewer set up ridiculous situations where, for example, a chair was positioned directly opposite the interviewer but with a huge pile of books on the table blocking the candidate from the interviewer, the idea being to produce something akin to the witch's "ducking stool"; it was impossible to win, and they only wanted to study the manner in which the candidate lost! If the candidate ignored the situation, he was challenged as to why he had; if the candidate moved the chair, the interviewer would challenge him on the basis that "we didn't ask you to come here to move the furniture around"; if the candidate asked the interviewer if he would move the books or if they could move the chair, he was attacked on the basis that "this is my office and I will lay it out any way I like."

Conduct of the interview

If you want to understand properly the principal characteristics and qualities of the candidate, then you need to conduct the interview according to a set of effective guidelines.

The questions should not dictate their own answers

If you want to find out whether, say, a candidate has had experience with a particular word processing program, you should not ask, "You have had experience with WordPerfect 5.0, haven't you?" The candidate is immediately told by this closed question that you are looking for someone with that experience; if she does not have it but is desperately trying to get the job she might be tempted to lie. In any case, you want to know what experience she considers to be most important before asking more specific questions about that experience. The question should therefore be open-ended and allow for the candidate to answer in her own style. You might ask, for example, "Could you tell us what word processing programs you have had experience with, and to what degree?"

The meaning of the question should be clear, taking into account the candidate's age and experience

You should set the questions according to the candidate and not according to yourself. The fact that you have an extensive experience and extensive vocabulary should not encourage you to show off those qualities to a 16-year-old candidate fresh from school. If you want the candidate to respond intelligently to your questions, they must be framed according to the probable background that the candidate might reasonably be expected to have had. You should also avoid asking questions in a manner that makes it difficult for those from ethnic minorities to understand or reply; such questioning could constitute indirect racial discrimination.

Probing questions should be used to examine and verify statements made by the candidate

The candidate will want to present himself in the best light; this is correct and proper but it should not be an excuse for the candidate to misrepresent himself. The candidate might, for example, say that he has had a great deal of experience working in inventory control. If that is relevant to this job then you should examine that statement with the question, "Could you tell us some of the detailed work you have done in that area?" Intelligent probing questions will determine whether the candidate has had five months' or five years' work in that department and whether he has a working knowledge of what is important and what he is bringing to this job.

The interviewer should control the direction of the interview

As we said earlier, the interview should run to a structure, though it should be a flexible one. By structuring the interview around preplanned key questions, you can keep the interview on track. Remember, however, to allow for flexibility in the questioning, depending on the responses of the candidate and other members of the interviewing panel, and remember to allow for the candidate to question you.

Avoid rude, insensitive, or irrelevant questions

As most secretaries are currently women, they will be familiar with the most common such question: "Can you tell us if you plan to get married and have a family in the next few years?" The most strikingly rude aspect of this question is that it would probably not be asked of a man, although the demands of marriage and a child could just as easily change his planned career path as it could a woman's. Such questions reveal hidden prejudices that you as an interviewer must ignore. Some rude, insensitive, or irrelevant questions could also be deemed to breach equal opportunity and race relations legislation.

Interviewers should not compare themselves to the candidate

You might well ask the candidate about her experience in, say, inventory control. When she makes it clear to you that she worked in the department for one year and handled accounts up to $50,000, that is relevant information for the interview. What would be completely irrelevant is for you to comment back, "Oh, I worked in inventory control for three years and I used to deal with accounts up to $250,000." Of what value is such a comment to the interview, the other members of the interviewing panel or the candidate? Does it help to assess whether the candidate is suitable for the job, or does it give the candidate information about the job in question? The answer to both is no. You might make comparisons if you feel that they help to build a bridge between you and the candidate or put the candidate at ease knowing there is a kindred spirit on the panel, but certainly there should be no more than a passing reference, after which you move on to a relevant discussion.

Do not judge the candidate's whole character or ability by one exceptional good or bad quality

It is very tempting to sell ourselves into or out of positions prematurely. For example, the candidate may say something that strikes you as insensitive or irrelevant and that you find somewhat inappropriate. Although this may give you a clue to the candidate's character, it may also be a reflection of stresses, and if you allow the impression gained to color your judgment throughout the whole interview, then you will possibly reject an otherwise very good candidate for the job.

Similarly, the candidate may have excellent experience, exactly as required for the job. Do not let that force you to conduct the interview from the viewpoint of "as far as I am concerned she has got the job unless I discover something very wrong." What this means is that you are no longer judging the candidate dispassionately but are in effect selling the candidate to yourself on her behalf and blinding yourself to other qualities; perhaps you would have discovered an inability to conduct herself well in teams.

Make notes after the interview, not during

Of course you will want to jot down some key words during the interview, particularly against your prepared main questions, but do not write copious notes of everything the candidate says. To do this will reduce the dynamics of the interview, create stress, and probably irritate the other members of the interviewing panel as well.

After the interview

Your company should have some sort of prepared interview exit form or report form that you have to complete to indicate your views about the candidate's education, experience, character, qualities, and so on. Assuming that it does (and it is presumably not your responsibility to prepare it—this job belongs to human resources), then make sure that you complete the form as soon as possible after the interview. Those arranging the interview should allow for a pause between each candidate to enable you to complete your summaries of each candidate as you go. If you try to save them all for the end of the day, when you come to complete the forms, your memory of each candidate will have blurred into one irretrievable conglomerate!

Remember too that you are seeking not the best, but the most suitable. Your comments should be graded from 1 to 5 on the following basis:
1. Considerably above average.
2. Above average.
3. Average.
4. Below average.
5. Considerably below average.

The most suitable candidate is probably one with qualities in band 3, the appropriate qualities for the job. Those at number 4 may be suitable but presumably will need some training or induction, and those at 2 may be suitable in the short term but will be seeking a career move very soon after joining you and will leave you if that career path is not available. Those at 1 are probably far overqualified for the job and will almost certainly leave you as soon as a better job is available. Those at 5 are too unqualified and the amount of training needed to bring them up to the appropriate standard is probably disproportionate and uneconomic. Remember that it is just as easy to be overqualified for a job as underqualified; neither candidate is suitable.

Staff Appraisal

Most companies recognize the value of regular monitoring of staff performance. Such monitoring, usually known as assessment or appraisal, is of great benefit not only to the company but also to the individual. As a member of, or leader of, the secretarial team, you will probably undergo staff appraisal and you may be involved in appraisal and appraisal interviews relating to those working for you.

The purposes of assessment or appraisal are as follows.

To identify levels of current performance

Each appraisal or assessment, probably done every six months or one year, should summarize the employee's current performance so that both the company and the employee have a measure of the contribution the employee is making to the workplace. With companies quite rightly identifying the value of synergy in team effort, such appraisals must also take into account the relationship of the employee to those working with him and whether or not the employee adds to or detracts from the morale and motivation of that team.

To identify improvements

Having determined the current position, the assessment or appraisal should also be looking toward those areas where the employee can improve performance levels.

To determine promotion

If staff are not offered the career track that they believe they are capable of, and want, then they will look for employment elsewhere and the company may lose its best staff. Therefore, the appraisal should also be looking toward what promotion might be wanted by the employee, what promotion might be available in the company, and of course what promotion is merited by the employee.

That said, the appraisal is not one-sided; it may be looking at what alternatives to promotion might be necessary. This could include transfer laterally to other departments or recognition that the employee is not performing to an acceptable standard, which could result in the employee being passed over by others who are performing to a more impressive degree.

To determine training needs

Most companies have recognized the value of training in that it develops current employees to their best potential and satisfies the needs of employees for personal development. The appraisal is used to determine what training is sought by the employee, needed by the employee, and recommended by the company. Such training could be refresher training for the job at hand, anticipatory training for changes in the job (e.g., technology changes), or training in anticipation of promotion.

To motivate the employee

Nothing is more demotivating than doing a good job, knowing you are doing a good job, and failing to have that recognized. "Appraisal" contains the word praise and it does not hurt to remember that the appraisal is a good time to add to the employee's motivation by commenting favorably on those areas where the employee has done well. It is also motivating, of course, for the employee to recognize that his training needs are being considered, his promotion and career track is under review, and so on.

To link levels of pay realistically to performance

Money is not necessarily a motivator, but the absence of money is highly demotivating. If people are not paid what they perceive themselves to be worth, they will feel aggrieved, become saboteurs within their own departments, and seek employment elsewhere. When the appraisal has been used to determine the current and future prospects of the employee, it should be used to make sure that the level of pay of the employee matches that position.

Note, however, that the appraisal interview should not itself be a discussion of salary or include this subject, for two reasons. First, it often becomes the dominant subject in the discussion and much of the value of the appraisal can be lost by concentrating on that one point. Second, if an employee is told his new salary at the appraisal interview, then it will be obvious to him that it had been determined before the interview and that all the important subjects discussed at the interview have not had an influence on that salary; this creates the impression of the appraisal being a sham.

Steps in performance appraisal

Whatever form of appraisal is going to be used, if you are going to be involved in the appraisal of your subordinates, and of course you will be involved in your own appraisal, then you should have a knowledge of the outline way in which your company deals with the subject. Many companies tend to let it happen in a rather *ad hoc* fashion, fitting in interviews randomly whenever they can and generally projecting a rather unprofessional image. This gives a subliminal impression of the appraisal as being of little importance. If you are being asked to assist in setting up appraisals in your department, then we would suggest you follow a series of stages similar to the following.

Stage 1

You and the member of your staff should agree on a time for the appraisal to take place, the objectives of the appraisal, and the main issues to be discussed. Your company should issue an appraisal form for whatever type of appraisal it undertakes, and we recommend that this is completed separately by you and the individual concerned. The comparison between the two is often enlightening.

Stage 2
The employee completes the appraisal form.

Stage 3
You should be gathering what information you require from various sources. You should also prepare for the appraisal interview, identifying key questions and points you will be raising. These will include current levels of performance, potential levels of performance, possible promotion (or alternatives), training needs, and so on.

Stage 4
Hold the appraisal interview with the employee. At this time, compare the appraisal forms you and the employee have completed and pay particular attention to areas where the two of you have very different views. It may be that the employee feels that he has done particularly well in some area and you feel, from discussion with the employee's colleagues as well as your own observations, that he has done particularly badly. Such differences often mean that the objectives of particular tasks have not been properly communicated.

Stage 5
Agree on new objectives for the future.

Stage 6
Prepare a report to be submitted to your boss, the personnel department, or whomever your department reports to. This should include recommendations that can be used by the personnel department to consider appropriate levels of pay raise, promotion, and so on.

We recommend that this report be discussed with the employee, possibly at a separate further interview; some companies prefer this to be kept confidential. Naturally you will have to keep to your company's regulations, but where you are given the opportunity for input, we would recommend that an open policy is highly motivating to the individual.

Types of appraisals
Different firms employ a variety of appraisal measures.

Ranking
An outdated and little-used system of employee appraisals takes all employees and ranks them in an order of merit. This says that number 1 is the best performer and number 10 is the worst performer. However, this is of practically no use to the employee or the company as it fails to show how much better the first is than the last and fails to identify the specific areas that can be developed in those that need training.

Grading
Grading works only in companies with very high numbers of employees. It works on the statistical basis that the majority of people will perform to an average level

(on the basis that that's what average means) and that certain other numbers of employees will be above and below that point. Grading forces the distribution into pre-set categories, such as:

Exceptional	10 percent
Above average	20 percent
Average	40 percent
Below average	20 percent
Poor	10 percent

You then take the 100 percent of employees, assess them on some numerical order, based on whatever criteria you have applied in the appraisal, and fit them according to numerical result into one of these categories.

The main drawback of grading systems is that when used alone, they do not identify overall improvements in the workforce or the overall improvement in the company as a result of increased recognition of training and so on. The system always has the same percentages and fails to recognize that the 10 percent poor this year could have been the 10 percent exceptional last year.

Rating scale

A rating scale is the same as a grading but with no preset quantities. As a result, you could have 100 percent of your staff as exceptional. This may seem contrary to the definition of exceptional but at least takes into account a situation where changes in the workforce as a result of training can be recognized. However, if you were to end up with a situation skewed to one end of the scale, it would probably require the company to adjust its own criteria for what constitute poor, average, and exceptional.

Open-ended or general

Open-ended or general appraisals contain written reviews by supervisors and managers, with no numeric quantification. Although this allows for great flexibility, it also allows for subjectivity, which can be misleading. In particular, a good employee can get marked down simply because she does not get along with the supervisor; this fails to recognize that there could be a problem with the supervisor's own interpersonal skills rather than with the employee's.

Behaviorally anchored rating scale (BARS)

Target point scores are listed against a set of criteria applied to all candidates. For example:

Works well under pressure	1	2	3	4	5
Positive influence on the team	1	2	3	4	5
Seeks opportunities	1	2	3	4	5
and so on.					

There may be as many as 50 such items on the list, all of which are applied to all the company's employees. Two copies of the BARS chart are issued as part of the appraisal form, one to the manager and one to the employee. Both should separately complete the BARS chart by circling the number they consider appropriate (1 is poor development, 5 is exceptional development).

The advantages of such a system are that it allows for comparison of employees across the board, automatically identifies areas where development training is required, and highlights areas of discrepancy where you and the employee circle significantly different numbers. The disadvantage of the system is that people have a tendency to circle the average box or one on either side. It takes a great deal to mark 1 or 5. Most BARS seem to use numbers 1 to 5, probably as they arise from the old grading systems, but if the scale runs from 1 to 6, then people at least cannot mark the average box, as there is no middle number.

Recommended appraisals

You will have to take part in whatever appraisal system your company has. However, in several training courses on this subject, delegates have indicated that they have been asked to set up formal appraisal systems in their departments. If that is the case, we would recommend a combination of BARS and written reviews. The appraisal form completed by both you and your member of staff should contain a written review of the employee's own development, the department's strengths and weaknesses, and any other areas thought to be important to the department, along with well thought out behavioral criteria for the BARS. A combination of the two allows for flexibility as well as quantifiable measures. The fact that both you and the employee are completing the same form allows for areas of difference to be easily identified; these are the areas on which future training or development are targeted.

Counseling in the Workplace

Essentially, counseling is a purposeful relationship in which one person helps others to help themselves. Counseling is almost exclusively done on a one-to-one basis with individuals.

As leader of the secretarial team, you will at various times be involved in counseling your staff through problems. These can be wide-ranging, including pressures resulting from the job itself, relationship problems in work, and difficulties that originate from outside work. If you are to be successful in being helpful to the employee, then there are a number of "dos" and "don'ts" to be considered.

There will be some problems where you are not qualified to assist and where you might ask the assistance of your medical department, if any, human resources department, and so on. There will also be areas that are too remote from the workplace and too complex to be within your limited counseling skills, such as marital difficulties, personal relationship problems outside work, and so on. You must remember that you are not primarily a counselor; you are a secretary and in this context the head of a secretarial department. There are therefore many more limitations on you than on an independent, professional counselor.

Although the needs of the employee must be met, you also have to recognize that the company is a place of work and not in itself a counseling office. You might suggest other sources of help if you have that information, or you might ask your personnel department to seek out assistance for your employee.

Take the view that you are using counseling techniques, rather than actually being a counselor. The major difference is that a counselor is committed to the person he is counseling, and free to discuss any issue. That cannot be, in practice, the case with you. If, for example, an employee came to you and confessed that she had falsified errors in the work of her colleagues with a view to decreasing their promotion possibilities and increasing her own, then you would almost certainly have the responsibility of reporting that more widely, probably to your personnel department. That is your corporate duty as the team leader responsible for the morale of your team and the promotion prospects of all members of your staff. This is clearly a limitation that would not be imposed on a professional counselor.

Use counseling techniques wisely but never forget your wider responsibilities to the company and to all the people around you.

The objectives of counseling

It is important to understand precisely what counseling is.

Helping people to recognize their own feelings

Many people's frustrations and difficulties arise from their own inability to understand why they feel the way they do about particular situations. Counseling helps people to recognize their own feelings by helping them to get in touch with, and understand, feelings they may have suppressed. For example, depression is often held to be suppressed anger, with the person not recognizing that he is angry, or not identifying what he is angry about.

Helping people to define problems

Quite often people know that there is a problem but do not know either what the problem is or how it has arisen. For example, a member of your team may come to you and tell you that she is unhappy in an open plan office environment because she cannot get along with the other five people in the room. This is causing the counselee anxiety and unhappiness. Although this is how the problem is likely to be presented to you, you can instantly see that this is very vague and ill-defined; it does not present a tangible situation that you can assist the counselee to find a solution to.

Your first task, therefore, is to help the individual to work out precisely what problems are causing the anxiety or unhappiness. For example: does the counselee believe that the other people in the room find her too chatty or not communicative enough; does she believe that she has few common interests with the other people in the room and feel excluded; does the counselee feel that those in the room treat her like the "office junior"; is there snobbery or elitism perceived in the situation? The goal of this aspect of counseling is to turn vague feelings into defined problems for which action can be considered.

Helping people to learn to live with the situation

With most problems, there are changes that can be made by the counselee or others that can change situations. Sometimes just repositioning a desk or making cosmetic changes to the office environment can improve morale, remotivate people, and so on. However, there are other cases where no change is possible and your job as a counselor is to help people to learn to live with that situation. For example, if the counselee comes to you and tells you that he feels unduly pressured by having to meet a deadline every Friday, there may be nothing that can be changed, in that the deadline has to be met as part of overall department responsibilities. Indeed, meeting that deadline is possibly one of the job responsibilities that were set out to him when he took the job in the first place. Of course, for any employee, there is always one major change available—to leave the job—but assuming that he is seeking a solution inside the company, in this instance the solution will be helping him to learn to live with the deadline.

You will have to help him to see the situation in a better perspective; he may be focusing on the negative aspects of his job (this deadline) and forgetting its very many positive aspects (work conditions, good salary). Consider changing his view of the Friday deadline; it may mean pressure on Friday but it also means he can go home with his work finished and have a pressure-free Saturday!

What is involved in counseling?

Counseling involves more listening than talking on the part of the counselor. For many people, just talking through their problems to you allows them to create their own solutions. Successful and useful counseling involves a great many dos and don'ts.

Giving advice

Giving advice is principally a don't. It is not your job in counseling to provide other people with solutions or to give them alternatives. For counseling to be effective, the counselees must own solutions by developing them themselves. There will of course be situations where it is sensible to offer some advice, but even then it should be in the form of a suggestion of alternatives from which the counselee can select her own chosen path.

Encouraging behavioral change

It is not the role of counseling to impose new behaviors or attitudes on individuals. It is the role of the counselor to help the individual to understand the variety of behaviors or attitudes available. At the same time, the counselor may have to point out which of those behaviors is unacceptable in the company. For example, if you are counseling someone who is known to be extremely aggressive in the office environment (she may have come to you with a problem and this has been identified between you, or you may have been asked to "have a word with the person" for this reason), then it is not for you to impose assertiveness training on her (though you might suggest it). However, it is for you to point out the differences between aggressiveness and assertiveness, to help the person to understand the differences in outcomes of the two approaches and to point out that the company will not accept aggressive behavior—and that if that is the path she chooses, then she will have to choose it outside the company.

Discussing problems

It is a clear "do" of counseling to be open in discussing problems with individuals; it is a clear "don't" to impose answers. Any answers must come from within the individual, though she is free to discuss possibilities with you.

Altering people's perception of a situation

It is quite clear that you should not impose your view of the situation on others. However, it is clear that you should help them to see the wider perspective, which will lead them to alter their own view of the situation.

Approaches to counseling

There are two approaches to counseling: the direct and the indirect.

Direct counseling

Direct counseling is now recognized as outdated and ineffective in the long term, though it may offer short-term solutions. Direct counseling is more in the way of advice giving and imposition and in that way is of more benefit to the team as a whole than to individuals. Direct counseling involves:

- outlining the consequences of various causes and actions;
- then suggesting a range of alternative solutions;
- then devising a path to the "correct" (i.e., counselor's) decision.

In this instance, the path is often devised by the so-called counselor, or possibly by the counselor and counselee in discussion. Furthermore, the "correct" decision is not only subjective but is often—in practice—the correct decision for the company or the department and not necessarily for the individual.

Direct counseling is not favored in the modern, and more enlightened, business environments where concern for the well-being of individuals is regarded as a responsibility, as well as a practical way of keeping people at their optimum performance levels.

Indirect counseling

Considered more effective, particularly in the longer term, is indirect counseling, which gets more to the root of the problem and creates a longer-term solution.

Indirect counseling:

- Recognizes that only the counselee is capable of accurately defining his own problem (it will take patience and an open relationship to get to this problem; the counselee may first present surface problems, and it may take time to dig down to the underlying difficulties).

- Allows for a discussion of what the counselee wishes to discuss; if he sets the agenda he will get to the heart of the problem more quickly (if you discuss what you want to discuss, even if that is directly related to the problems arising in the office, you may miss the underlying causes, which possibly only the counselee is aware of).
- Recognizes that counselees must be fully behind any solution if it is to work (you cannot impose attitudinal behavioral changes; they must come from the counselee).
- Recognizes that counselees must feel they can rely on the expertise and experience of the counselor, but that the counselee must make the final decisions. (You may have a wider experience of office-based problems, you may even have tried and tested solutions, but as before you cannot impose these; the counselee must seek them out for himself or herself with your help, and from a range of alternatives. The counselee must be encouraged to search for alternatives.)

Environments that encourage or inhibit counseling

Counselors need to be aware of their own behaviors and attitudes, which can encourage or inhibit effective counseling.

Behaviors and attitudes that encourage counseling	Behaviors and attitudes that inhibit counseling
Building trust and respect	Being too rigid and formal
Openness	Seeking to control others
Empathy	Feeling defensive
Acceptance (nonjudgmental)	Unable to accept criticism
Giving feedback	Narrow thinking
Accepting feedback	Being unadaptable
Acknowledging the feelings of others	Imposing solutions
Recognizing the rights of others	Not being aware of the feelings of others
Valuing initiative	
Valuing creativity	Giving personalized, vague criticism
Being open to radical suggestions/ solutions	Giving overgeneralized feedback
Accepting that error and failure are learning opportunities	Interrupting
Being supportive	Impatience
Giving praise	Withholding information
Offering constructive criticism	Feeling uneasy about the process of counseling
Confidence	
Making time for the counseling process	Begrudging time taken for counseling

Effective approaches to counseling

The way you speak and the way you act while counseling have an effect on the counselee.

Effective, positive verbal behaviors include the following:

- Use the counselee's name. Be sure to address the counselee by name, as a person, rather than treating her like an object. Use her name throughout the conversation to reinforce this ("That was a good suggestion, Susan"). Where appropriate, use the counselee's first name.
- Allow counselees time to have their say. Be patient.
- Paraphrase and feed back what they have said. This ensures that you have understood their meaning accurately and gives them a chance to correct your misapprehensions if you have misjudged their meaning.
- Verbally acknowledge their views and ideas. Let them know that you understand their point of view.
- Be open. Ask open-ended questions that allow counselees to answer in their own way rather than asking questions that demand a particular direction of reply. Be receptive to the counselees' responses.
- Stick to the issue. Help the counselee to focus on the main problem by reflecting back important points from her dialogue.
- Appropriate response. Counselors should respond to the person, rather than trying to concentrate on giving a good response.

Nonverbal behaviors include the following:

- Stand or sit beside the counselee, not across a desk creating a barrier. Remember that as the counselor you do not want to have a dominating or imposing position over the counselee, e.g., you do not want to stand while the counselee sits.
- Keep an open and relaxed posture. You should not feel the need to be aloof (e.g., arms crossed across the chest) or defensive (e.g., arms crossed low down on the torso). Your relaxed posture will encourage relaxation in the counselee.
- Maintain assertive, comfortable eye contact. Behaviors tend to breed behaviors; assertive body language encourages assertiveness in the counselee.
- Demonstrate that you are listening. Apart from intelligent feedback (verbal) to determine comprehension, you should demonstrate you are listening throughout the counselee's speeches by nodding, leaning forward, and so on.
- Smile appropriately. You should smile at appropriate times, openly and genuinely.

Summary

Counseling involves first exploring problems, then understanding them, and finally—and only after the first two—discussing a course of action. Never be tempted to consider solutions before you and the counselee feel confident that you fully understand the real problems.

Repetitive Strain Injury (RSI)

Repetitive strain injury is the name given, in the case of secretaries working with display screen equipment, to the discomfort and more serious pains that can arise from routine regular use of keyboards. Although news coverage of RSI tends to focus on secretarial use, it is a wider-ranging term relating to soft tissue injuries. Carpal tunnel syndrome, tennis elbow, and so on are included in these disorders.

Repetitive strain injury is believed to be caused by a number of contributory factors:

- *Force.* The fingers are not designed to take a lot of high impact and are easily susceptible to strain.
- *Repetition.* It is not specifically known why repetitive movements create strain but it is recognized that for the muscles to retain their flexibility and for the tendons to retain their lubrication, a variation in movement is needed.
- *Posture.* Although you may not be moving your body, you might be using your muscles. In fact, muscles work very hard to hold a static position, and are "easiest" when moving. Therefore a rigid position of back and legs and parts of the arm while keystroking causes muscle strain, whereas a more relaxed, flexible posture reduces it.
- *Rest.* Changes of posture and changes of focus of attention by planned breaks reduce the possibility of RSI.

Identifying RSI

RSI comes in a variety of intensities and you should identify the potential risk as soon as possible in order to minimize severe damage.

- *Mild.* This is identified by aches, pains, and tiredness in the wrists, arms, shoulders, or neck during work. Once you leave work, the pain goes away. Depending on the work environment, this can last for several weeks at a time but can be reversed.
- *Moderate.* Where the aching pains and tiredness are recurrent and occur not only at work but also during the night, even disturbing sleep, then RSI is becoming moderately serious. There may be some physical signs, such as swelling of the wrist. This can last for several months but is still at this stage reversible.
- *Severe.* Even when resting, even when not at work—perhaps on vacation—the pains and fatigue in the arms are still apparent. Sleep is often disturbed during these periods, which can last for years. Sometimes RSI damage is irreversible and full comfort and use of the arms is never regained.

Obviously it is in everyone's interest to reduce RSI risk by identifying the onset of it at the earlier stage and making appropriate adjustments to workstation, display screen equipment, and work routines in order to deal with it. The following actions are recommended:

- avoid prolonged work in the same position;
- vary work activity as much as practical;
- avoid extreme movements and stretching;
- take varied rest breaks, preferably at times of your own choice;
- consider job rotation in order to increase variation of tasks;
- consider workstation layout;
- key stroke at a comfortable rate;
- encourage training and awareness of RSI and symptoms;
- report RSI symptoms immediately.

Victims of RSI have had more than their work affected: one secretary reported such agony that she could neither brush her teeth nor comb her hair; another suffered severe pins and needles in her arm and wrist, resulting in many weeks off from work, and so on. There have also been some considerable financial settlements. One electronics worker suffering from RSI received compensation of $20,000, six factory workers received $21,000, and an automobile plant machine operator was awarded almost $60,000.

The fact that there have been compensation payouts should be warning enough for employers and the fact that it is widely reported—whether it is physical, psychological, or physiological—means that it is a condition that needs addressing at some level. We would recommend that workstation commonsense points should be implemented. RSI or not, they increase the secretary's comfort, improve working conditions, and provide for higher quality performance.

PART 2

Time Management for the Boss–Secretary Partnership

The modern secretary has all the usual time management problems of business life, but the added complication of managing not just her own time but also that of the boss. In this section, we shall be looking at the boss–secretary partnership and the ways in which recognizing it as a partnership can be of great benefit to both.

Before we get to practical time management steps, it is worth considering the strange lack of value that we put on time.

Value Tests

Consider that you have just won a lottery. Your prize is $1 million. Imagine that, as you are reading this book, the door opens and our representative puts on the table in front of you a briefcase with $1 million in it. It is yours to do with what you will. So what will you do with it?

This is an exercise we do in our training programs and the most common answers are as follows:

- buy a new, bigger, house;
- have a long, exotic vacation;
- buy a whole new wardrobe of clothes;
- indulge in pampering health care;
- buy a very expensive car (a sports car is usually suggested);
- buy much wanted items for the family (a new house for parents.)

There are also a number of sensible answers offered, such as investing the money and living off the interest or creating a trust for children. However, it always seems that these suggestions are offered with a little less conviction; perhaps a desire to be seen to be practical and sensible. The brainstorming discussions that we have had indicate that most people have a very strong desire to be indulgent and frivolous.

However, what happens if we change your prize? In this strange lottery, you have no longer just won the $1 million; this time it comes with strings. You can have the million but you can never have any more money at any time during your life. You cannot earn more, steal more, marry more, inherit more, or earn interest. From this day forward your $1 million is all that you will ever have. How does that change the answers to our question, "What are you going to do with the money?"

Invariably the sensible answers such as investment programs go straight to the top of the list. Even the so-called frivolous answers become modified; e.g., a bigger house but not an extravagant one, or a really good vacation, but not the world cruise. What does this mean?

It means that when we begin to appreciate the value of a scarce resource, we seek to control it by creating budgets. When the $1 million is found money, extra to the normal expected money for which we have created budgets in our life, we feel free to be extravagant. But when the money represents all that we will have, we seek to control it for the budget.

This can be demonstrated by two further offers that we have made to training delegates. Imagine that our representative comes into your room, puts a briefcase on the table, offers you all the money that is in the briefcase, and says that you can never have any more than what is there. The catch this time is that you do not know how much is in the briefcase. It could be $500 million, it could be $5. Would you take the deal? We have not yet had a positive reply in our training sessions; no one is prepared to take the risk. The delights of $500 million are clearly significantly outweighed by the possibility of finding yourself with $5 with which to survive for the rest of your life. And quite rightly so; such an offer highlights the value we place on money.

A further attitudinal test concerns a similar briefcase placed in front of you with a slot in the side and a $10 bill sticking out of it. It is the same offer as before. You can have all the money in the briefcase but you don't know how much is in there. You can tear off the $10 bill and spend it; as soon as you have spent it another $10 bill will appear, and this will continue. However, there will come a time when the $10 bill will not appear and the money will have run out. Would you take *that* deal?

Again, we have not yet had a single person in our training sessions who has thought it a good deal, or who has said he will take it. Yet when we transpose money for time, that is exactly the deal that every one of us took the day we were born. We live a minute (we spend that minute), another minute appears (and we spend that minute), and we keep on going until the time comes when we use a minute and another one does not appear after it.

So if we look at the processes above and replace money with time, we realize that we are living a life with time allocated in exactly the way we would wish it not to be. But that is life. What we have to do is learn to appreciate the value of time in the way that we have learned to appreciate the value of money. In fact, we should learn to value time more because money does not act only in the way described, but can be more flexible.

Consider now a last attitude test on the value we place on money as opposed to the value we place on time. Instead of our representative with his generous briefcase, the person who comes into the room where you are is a thief, who runs across the room, grabs your bag containing your purse or wallet and runs off with it. You will try to apprehend him. You will almost certainly call the police, and if the thief is caught, you will probably press charges for theft. Yet the amount stolen could be only a few dollars. It is rarely the amount that concerns us so much as the principle of being a victim of a thief. Yet that totally inelastic and irreplaceable commodity of which we have an unknown amount, we allow to be stolen every day by thieves who come into our offices and steal our time. And we would not for a moment consider prosecuting anyone for what is in fact a much more serious theft. The time bandits are examined beginning on page 66.

In this section, we will be looking at practical steps for time management in the office, at our workplace, and in our everyday life. Some of these are well-known techniques—prioritization, listing—but all of these are very uninspiring and very unsatisfying if they are not supported by a change in our attitude to time that recognizes its immense value.

We approach this by dividing our time management into two areas:

- "diary-based" time management for routines and procedures;
- "goal-based" time management to create the framework for our lives (at home and at work).

How We Spend Our Life

If we assume an average life span of 70 years, it can be quite shocking to realize how those 70 years go by. The following is an average analysis of the statistical use made by Western Europeans or North Americans.

Activity	Number of years
Sleep	25
Work and school	17
Eating	7
Bathroom	1.5
Travel (getting nowhere)	2.5
Dressing	1
Waiting	1.5
Medical: hospitals, doctors	5
Leisure options	
Watching TV	6
Visiting others	2
Sundries (hobbies)	6
Total	74.5

Some comments on this are required. The work and school years can, more commonly in the case of women, be made up of housework and school. Indeed, for many women, the sundries years can also be made up of household-related tasks. A great deal of time is literally wasted: the years of travel getting nowhere represent travel to and from work or to and from places of habit, not travel for pleasure's sake. The years of "waiting for something" are equally regarded as wasted rather than time spent enjoying the environment. Incidentally, and it is outside the scope of this book, studies of sleep indicate that the 25 years we spend sleeping may be a great waste, as sleep is often just a habit and can be reduced considerably for many people.

It is perhaps daunting to consider that out of our entire life only 14 years are available for use at our own discretion, and if the six years contained in "sundries" is spent on household-related tasks, then only eight years are discretional. And the average person spends six of those watching the television!

As an exercise on the value of money, we applied our $1 million to the 14 years that you have the option to spend. Fourteen years represents 5,110 days, each day being worth $195.70. If, for example, you had watched every episode of 30 years of *Guiding Light* (based on the old schedules of two half-hour programs per week) then you would have spent 1,560 hours, or 65 days at $195.70 ($12,720.50). You must ask yourself, if you had $1 million to spend and no more for the rest of your life, would you spend $12,720.50 of it to watch *Guiding Light?* For the whole six years spent watching television, you would have spent $428,571 out of your $1 million.

Figure 4 shows a time voucher. It is drawn on your bank of personal time, i.e., the bank in which you have the time equivalent of $1 million—and no more—and a balance that can only go down. Every time you spend some time, consider whether you would be happy to write a voucher drawing from your bank of personal time. Keep it with you when you are traveling, watching TV, lying on the sofa staring at the ceiling, wondering what to do, and so on.

THE BANK OF PERSONAL TIME

DATED: ....

PAY TO:...

THE AMOUNT OF: ....
     (in words)

FOR:..

Signature: ....

Hours	Mins

Figure 4 Time voucher.

We Are Not Taught to Manage Time

We have demonstrated that people have a very curious attitude to the inelasticity and irreplaceability of time. Where does this cavalier attitude to time come from, considering our often rigid attitude to money? The evidence is that the following contribute to our views.

We are taught that time is infinite

Philosophical arguments aside, time probably is infinite. It has existed since the creation of the universe and will exist to its end. We talk about the dinosaurs having lived for 150 million years, dying out 65 million years ago, about humans having been on earth for a few million years, and so on. These are big numbers, but meaningless in any sensible context. We live for approximately 70 years and that is the very final measure with which we have to work. We should cease to think of time as something infinite (therefore uncontrollable and not in need of budgeting) and regard it as something scarce. Scarcity always increases the value of a commodity and many people need an understanding of time based on its scarcity.

We teach children the value of money but we do not teach the value of time

Mathematics is often taught to young children at school in a practical environment where, for example, the school may set up a store with various items (building bricks, pencils, model fruit) priced at various prices (10 cents, 25 cents, 50 cents, and so on). The children are told that they have X cents to spend, that they must buy three things and get Z cents in change. The children then have to work out how to get what they want and retain some money. While learning mathematics, they are also learning, albeit subconsciously and even unintentionally, about value for money, saving versus spending, and so on. But we never teach them mathematics using values of time.

When we spend children's time for them, we do so in a way that undervalues time and creates the subliminal message that it is something not to be quantified, valued, or spent wisely. We tell them, for example, "Go out and play." Play is of course highly valuable and should be encouraged, but we are referring to the tone of voice that indicates that they should in reality "get out from under our feet and go away and do anything they like except annoy us." Or we tell them "Go and watch TV," not because there is some highly educational or highly entertaining program on but because we want to keep their minds occupied while we get on with talking to our friends, having a quiet cup of coffee, or sleeping/medical things/sundry hobbies with our spouse.

The value of money is therefore reinforced, and the valuelessness of time is equally reinforced.

Our first exposure to time management

In school, we are first exposed to time management when we face the prospect of exams. Here we see the beginning of the attitude change necessary to make time management practical and enjoyable. We must recognize that exams are a goal-based time management project. We know when we are to take the exam; we subtract that point in time from the point in time at which we presently are and this gives us a period of time over which we can plan and budget our studying. But it is not the time spent studying that is our focus; the focus is the goal at the end.

Many people who have bad time management problems have them because they cannot see how their routines fit into their goals, usually because they have no formalized goals. Part of good time management is to have a goal-making structure (see Goal Setting, beginning on page 58).

The goal of routine tasks could be said to be effectively controlling tasks such as paperwork, filing, and so on. For the time being, we can accept this as correct although later we will make clear the distinction between goal-based and diary-based management techniques.

Events in life that give pain, pleasure, and satisfaction are not time-based

Memory does not recall time accurately. For example:

- What were you doing on Christmas Day 1987?
- Where were you on March 28, 1989?
- What were you doing at 7:30 P.M. last Saturday?
- Where were you on February 14, 1988?
- What were you doing at 2:30 P.M. on this day, last week?

The chances are that you do not know because the date is irrelevant. It may offer clues, because you might know what you were doing on most Christmas Days in the past few years, but the chances are you could not specifically be sure what you were doing on Christmas Day in 1987, and so on.

However, your memory does operate on a goal (event) basis. For example, you might well know the answers to the following questions:

- What was your most enjoyable car journey?
- Can you recall the last time you did your favorite hobby?
- Can you recall the last time you redecorated your home?
- What was memorable about the best meal you ever had?

In the case of the last time you redecorated your home, what you can remember about it is likely to be the pain and pleasure you had and the eventual result. Unless you had to fit it in to your work vacations, it is unlikely that you could remember exactly how long the work took. By the same token, if the most memorable thing about the best meal you ever had was the time it took to eat it then, sadly, you have had some very unmemorable meals.

In fact, the only time we are aware of time passing is when we are bored, and not giving of our best.

If we learn to think in terms of goal-based time management for the broad structure in which we run our lives, then we can begin to build exciting and practical goals that give our lives purpose and meaning. Without such purpose and meaning, even the cleverest time planning techniques become a chore rather than a pleasurable part of our lives.

Do not undervalue the need for goals and challenges in our lives. So many people with so much potential in our training courses have demonstrated that the one thing they lack, and in many cases they have worked this out for themselves, is a purposeful direction. They feel themselves drifting along, bobbing up and down on the waves caused by other people's passing ships. Sometimes that lack of purposefulness is extreme. In August 1994, a student who had continually told friends that he was bored laid his head down on a railway track and died when hit by a train. He had spelled out in large letters in stone next to him the word "bored." His father indicated that there had been insufficient challenge provided for him.

Red Time and Green Time

We have been suggesting changes to the way we value time. To make these practical, we suggest you think in terms of red time and green time. Before we explain the difference, consider the following. You are lying on the sofa staring at the ceiling for half an hour. Is this red time or green time?

The answer is: it could be either. It depends on why you are doing it. If you are lolling on the sofa staring at the ceiling because you cannot think of anything else to do and you are bored out of your mind, then you are very firmly living in red time. However, if your half hour is relaxation you have always sought, and if you have given it to yourself as a reward for achievements in meeting targets and goals, and perhaps most importantly, if you are enjoying it rather than fretting about it, then you are living in green time. From this, we can define the two:

- Red time is time wasted, i.e., time not spent achieving our desires, targets, goals.
- Green time is time well spent, i.e., toward our goals.

We are not from the school of writing or training that says you are only doing something useful in life if you are jogging around the block while reading a scientific treatise and working out how to save the global environment. The good news for delegates in our training courses is that if the situation is right, we are more than happy to recommend relaxation and quietness, and even time spent watching TV. And an active, busy person is living in red time if the effort is getting that person no nearer to her desired goals.

Your goal is to live totally in green time. Both authors of this book made that their principle some years ago and, with the rare hiccup, we have achieved it. Apart from planning time aimed toward specific targets or goals, the trick of living in green time is first to work out what your potential red time is and then to have both a plan and a contingency for dealing with it, i.e., converting it to green time. Consider the following situations:

1. Two hours commuting each day.
2. Doing the ironing.
3. Doing yard work.
4. Playing with your children.
5. Falling asleep on the train home and waking up at the wrong station at two o'clock in the morning, with perhaps no more trains that night.

We have suggested to delegates that these are red time situations and asked them how they would convert them to green time.

Two hours commuting each day

You might of course decide that you can achieve the goal of improving your quality of life by changing jobs and not commuting in this way. But for many people, and virtually everyone working in major cities, a significant amount of commuting is inevitable. The conversion of that commuting into green time could be achieved by, say, using it for studying for some qualification. Some Long Island Railroad services were innovative in this area some years ago, and set aside certain cars for people to take classes during the long commute to New York City.

You might argue that you use the time to read the newspaper or a novel and that might well be green time. However, ask yourself whether you read the novel or the newspaper just to pass the time or whether you read it because it is important to you that you do.

Ironing

The routine maintenance of our lives, whether it is at home doing the ironing, cleaning up, or clothes washing, or in the office doing filing, paperwork, and so on, cannot be avoided and should not be regarded as entirely red time. However, there are two approaches to making it more green time.

The first is to acknowledge that some tasks, for you, are totally red time and you must decide not to do them. In the case of the chores at home, you might hire someone else to come to your home and do it; you might have to take a small part-time job, perhaps in the evening, or working from home, to pay for that. In the case of office-based chores, if you decide you simply cannot tolerate them, then you must acknowledge that you are in the wrong job and you must begin looking for a job that suits you better. And you should make that job search a goal (see Goal Setting, beginning on page 58).

The second approach for many people is to accept that they have tasks to be done and not to regard them as red time, but to increase the green time content of them. In this instance, there are two approaches. You can swap tasks (at home, "You do the ironing, I'll do the shopping"; in the office, "You do this photocopying, I'll do some of your typing"). The latter case demands a company culture that allows for such choices (we will look at alternatives to delegation later). The other approach is to combine routine tasks where possible. In the case of the ironing, you might like to take in one news broadcast every evening and although these are on the television, they are not usually essentially visual. You can therefore do the ironing while listening to the news, because they are dealt with differently in the brain (one intellectually absorbed, the other a routine task often done on autopilot).

Yard work

All that is described above in respect to ironing could apply to yard work. However, we have isolated this activity in order to introduce an extraordinary but real case history we came across. One couple had accepted that they wanted a yard for their children to play in, and grow up in, but neither of them enjoyed gardening. They came to the conclusion that the most effective course of action was to hire a gardener, which they did. Maintenance and other work in the yard became quite costly, landscaping work in particular, and the only way to support the situation was for both of them to seek better paying jobs. Spurred on by the goal of needing the money, they successfully got better jobs that led to them being able to get an increased mortgage and to move to a larger house. In the larger house, they could not keep their jobs and maintain the house and yard and therefore, in addition to the gardener, they had to hire a cleaning lady and a nanny. For a variety of related reasons, they ended up with more than one car each, needing long-distance commuting cars, shopping cars, and a van for taking the children and friends to school. As a result, they had to have an extended garage built and some front yard was given over to extended parking. They created a small business to provide a little extra money. That business was very successful, partly because—they believe—they exhibited the trappings of wealth: a large house, several cars, and live-in help. Consequently, they were able to move to an even larger house where the cycle appears to be continuing. They are quite certain in their minds that the push that created the situation came originally from dealing with the problem of how to make the gardening green time. (This is also a useful example of a principle we have demonstrated many times in other training courses: that we do not, as conventionally thought, spend what we earn, but rather we earn what we spend. In other words, if we set our sights a little higher on the things we want to spend our money on, then we find ways to stretch our money to meet those demands, or inspire ourselves to get pay increases, or better paid jobs.)

Playing with your children

If ever we had evidence of a difference in attitude between men and women, it comes from putting this allegedly red time situation on the flip chart. In our various courses, we have suggested this to groups of secretaries, predominantly female, and groups of managers, with a higher proportion of men. The men generally will discuss turning playing with their children into green time and come up with some very creative ideas, such as making sure that the games played are a training ground for future jobs for their children, or that the game in some way allows the father to do some work he has brought home from the office. The groups of women immediately challenge the suggestion on the basis that playing with your children is green time and should not be regarded as red time. In our training courses, once the men have finished creating their green time ideas, we put it to them that playing with the children ought to be green time anyway, and not regarded as red time. There are usually a few embarrassed faces and a general agreement.

We would of course suggest that if you regard playing with your children as red time, you should make the effort to reevaluate your priorities in life.

Falling asleep on the train at two in the morning

There are going to be times, such as in this example, when accidents happen and you are not in planned time. The simple answer to turning unplanned accidents into green time is always to have contingencies with you. The authors of this book, for example, always make it a principle to carry with them work that needs doing, such as papers from our reading tray (see page 98), course or manuscript outlines, or drafts that need working through. When accidents happen (trains break down, people are late for appointments, you arrive earlier than expected for meetings) then there is constructive work to be done.

In the case of the example given, if you have material with you, then you can use this while getting yourself back home or in any waking time during an enforced overnight stay. More radically, you can decide that it is time to use the opportunity to pamper yourself as you have been promising to do, book yourself into a luxury hotel, and make sure you enjoy all its facilities. (The only inevitable red time component here would be spending time working out how to make your spouse believe your story!)

Goal Setting

The last aspect of changing your attitude toward time is to have a series of goals that form the structure of your life, and the broad reasons for the things you do. Without goals, even the most efficient time manager is constantly plagued by a feeling of dissatisfaction with her life.

We suggest a perpetual program of three stages of goals. By this, we mean that as certain goals are achieved, others must then replace them, and certain goals will be deflected. We would point out that the fact that you make a decision to stop pursuing a goal that has driven you so far does not make it irrelevant. The fact that the goal has driven you so far means it has served its purpose. Every goal does not have to be achieved for your life to be meaningful, but each goal must be held with a view to achievement. The three stages of goals are as follows.

Six-month goals

You should have short-term goals designed to achieve your objectives over a six-month period. These will typically include:

- I will have the backlog in my filing tray cleared in two weeks time.
- I will rearrange that filing system I have been meaning to rearrange for the past two years within three months.
- I will finalize that proposal for a new word processing package that I have been meaning to show to my boss over the past year, and present it within four months.
- I will make sure that the spare room at home is decorated within six months.
- I will make sure that I have cleaned out the kitchen drawer and tidied it up within one month.

These six-month goals are often more in the manner of targets: specific tasks with specific deadlines to be met. There is one further six-month goal that is important: I will achieve within six months the short-term sections of my longer term goals (see below).

The two further goal settings we suggest are longer term, and making them practical and achievable relies on breaking them up into "bite-sized chunks," each of which then becomes a short-term target within the long-term goal. These must be taken into account in your short-term goal setting.

Five-year goals

We suggest that you hold up a crystal ball (in your mind, or in reality if you have one) and look into it to see your own future. What do you see? Do you see yourself sitting in a bigger office? Or a bigger house? Or a better decorated version of your existing house? Or do you see an entirely different lifestyle based on a change of job? And so on. Focus on those images that you want to happen: Do you want a different job, a promotion, a bigger house? If you decide that you do, then you must make it part of your green time goal setting that you should always be doing something toward that goal.

If you want a promotion then you must break down your five-year plan (or two-year plan, or whatever) into six-month chunks and you must make sure that you achieve targets aimed at the goal. For example, in the first six months, you might decide that you must have examined all the possible opportunities for your type of work within your company, and possibly in other companies, and make sure that you know what is involved in getting those jobs. Do you need more training? Do you need more experience before the job will be available to you? Having decided, you should have other specific targets for the next six months, e.g., obtaining for yourself the necessary training or putting yourself in a position where you can gain the experience. Do not let this just be a hope that it will happen; the whole point about goal setting is it must be in your control and you must make the effort to make sure that the times you spend are aimed at those goals. Therefore, if your five-year plan is to get promoted and your shorter-term goals include having to obtain a particular qualification, then you might combine these with turning your commuting into green time by studying for that qualification while commuting.

You should always be asking yourself, particularly if faced with potential red time, "Could I be doing something right now that is working toward my longer-term goals?" In fact, you should always be asking yourself, "Am I doing the things that are necessary to achieve the goals?" If you are not, or if you are holding the goal intangibly in front of you but merely hoping that it will happen one day, then you are not goal setting, you are dreaming. We are not trying to take away your dreams; but you might bear in mind that the only people who ever achieve their dreams are those who convert them into practical achievable goals and set about a deliberate course of action designed to make their dreams come true.

Tombstone goals

We suggest that you also have very long-term goals in mind, which, although they will change throughout your life, are the background tapestry against which all of your life is dictated at any given time. The success or failure of those goals could be considered to be your epitaph. Imagine that you have finally turned up your toes and applied for a receptionist's position at the Pearly Gates. What is written on your tombstone? Is it:

"He was quite pleasant and fairly competent at his job?" Or is it:

"She was the nicest millionaire who ever lived?"

Neither might be right for you but you might want your tombstone to reflect achievement rather than a lifetime of boredom and nonachievement. Consider that your tombstone should tell the world that you had goals that made you and those around you feel that you had fun, that you contributed to the world in a variety of ways, and that you achieved those goals. One delegate offered one of the authors a tombstone for himself that said:

I have spent my life training people
to use their time more effectively;
why are you standing here
reading my tombstone?

If you have accepted the message so far, then you should have considered at least some changes in your attitude to time and its value. We hope that even at this stage, you are beginning to think of the broad structure that you want for your life, into which day-to-day time management, which now follows, can be fitted. As you read on, remember that we shall be looking at two aspects of goal setting and time management: what might be called project goals, i.e., specific budgets and deadlines that need to be met; and maintenance goals, such as filing and typing, where the job is never finished but must be managed.

The Grid of Urgency

Pareto's law tells us that 80 percent of activity produces 20 percent of the results, whereas 20 percent of activity can produce 80 percent of results. It is therefore logical to focus on the 20 percent that produces the most results if we are to achieve more performance with less effort. This involves separating the few vital tasks from the many trivial and devoting resources to those vital tasks.

We can do this through a "grid of urgency," which identifies tasks that are: important and urgent; important but not urgent; urgent but not important; and neither urgent nor important. The grid of urgency is set out in Figure 5.

As you can see from the grid, the question of who does tasks, and when they are done, can be planned. Urgent and important tasks have to be done now and probably either directly by you or under your fairly close supervision. You may decide that you have to do important but not urgent tasks but you should now be thinking, "When is the most appropriate time to complete this task?" If the task is urgent but not important, then although you must decide that it has to be done now you might decide that you can delegate it to others without close supervision, and your question becomes one of who should be doing the task. If the job is neither urgent nor important, but if you decide that it still has to be done, then you should still identify a person to do the task and ask him to build it into his time planner, treating it as a target to be dealt with. Such tasks can of course be delayed if more urgent tasks arise in the meantime.

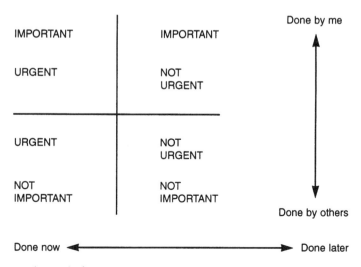

Figure 5 The grid of urgency.

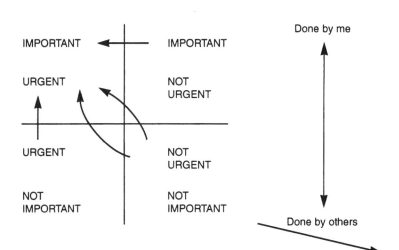

Figure 6 The grid of urgency showing the effects of procrastination and ineffective prioritization.

A grid of urgency is best understood with the addition of five arrows, as shown in Figure 6. These arrows demonstrate the way in which the priority of tasks can change if they are ignored. Urgent but not important tasks, and important but not urgent tasks, will become both important and urgent if they are not dealt with. Similarly tasks that are presently not urgent or important will gradually move through the boxes for important but not urgent or urgent but not important and if left continually will eventually arrive in the important and urgent box.

Picking up on the point above, if a task is not urgent and not important and never likely to move toward being important and urgent if it is ignored, then the question you should be asking is not who should do it, or when they should do it, but whether it should be done at all. Our desks are often cluttered up by jobs that we, in some subconscious way, know we will never do anyway and part of time management is to have the courage to pick them up and throw them in the garbage pail today rather than tomorrow, freeing our desks and our minds from thinking about them. If the old adage "never put off until tomorrow what you can do today" has validity, then we feel that there is at least equal validity in "never put off until tomorrow that which you can forget about completely." The fifth arrow leading off to the bottom right in Figure 6 is therefore aimed at your wastepaper basket!

What are the effects of these arrows? On paper, they seem to reclassify the jobs as increasingly important or urgent and this is true. However, consider how that fits into the grid of urgency: it also means that the longer tasks are left, the more likely it is that they will have to be done in a crisis (now!) and by you rather than someone else. Your procrastination, or your allowing others to procrastinate, will increase pressure on you. The quicker you get to grips with the grid of urgency and, using techniques set out in this book, make sure that other people get to grips with it too, the quicker your own time management will become more controlled.

The identification of which box tasks should, at least initially, go into can best be explained by examples:

- *Important and urgent.* Tasks that must be done by you, and done now. These might include preparing a particularly important presentation that will win a contract, sending out a very important letter, perhaps on behalf of your boss who is temporarily absent from the office, or clearing the building in the event of a fire.
- *Urgent but not important.* Must be done now but not necessarily by you. Such tasks might include a less important letter that, nonetheless, must go out tonight, perhaps to meet a deadline; or the issue of a memo giving people information about new parking arrangements that start on Monday next week. (If the memo doesn't go out now, it will soon be too late but on the other hand, the effect of it not going out is unlikely to have any serious repercussions.)
- *Important but not urgent.* Tasks that might have to be done by you, but not necessarily immediately. These might include your boss's personal filing, a health and safety memo not requiring implementation for several weeks, and so on.
- *Not important and not urgent.* Probably done by others, and can be done later, or possibly not bothered with at all. Such tasks might include putting little stickers on the filing cabinets or rearranging the stationery drawer.

Priorities

The grid of urgency allows you to classify tasks in a way that leads you to prioritize them. Clearing tasks from your desk using the grid of urgency demands, of course, that you give priority attention to urgent and important tasks, with others ranking in lower priority. You will arrange your filing trays to reflect these priorities (see page 100). You must then be disciplined and make sure that you clear tasks in the priority order. We all have a tendency to do the tasks we enjoy doing, or the easy tasks, before taking on the difficult or unrewarding ones, but we must be disciplined enough to recognize that sometimes the unrewarding ones or the unpleasant ones are the ones that have to be done. Putting them off creates crisis management.

However, priorities can change, particularly in the situation where you are subject to your boss's view of his own priorities, and of course your boss's view of your priorities. Throughout this section, we will be looking at the way you should be building a working partnership with your boss. The first aspect of that is priority setting.

Some priorities are just a habit

What time of day do you open the mail? The chances are that most companies open their mail first thing in the morning. Why? In some cases, people may be working in an immediate environment, such as the placing of insurance, where time is of the essence. Those companies might want to react to letters fairly immediately.

Many companies do not have that level of urgency and because that will be known, anyone seeking to attract the company's attention with urgency will probably use the telephone or fax; therefore the mail is not of immediate urgency. Yet, in many companies, the mail is usually opened first thing in the morning, distributed around the offices, and dealt with over a period of several days. So why open it in the morning rather than at three o'clock in the afternoon, which, in your company, just could be the most appropriate time? The answer is because the mailman delivered the mail the first thing in the morning and we all have a tendency to open our mail as soon as we receive it. But this is not good time management; it means that a fairly major task that is routinely dealt with every day is being planned according to the whims of the post office and the mailman rather than because it suits you, your department, and your company.

It may be that first thing in the morning is the appropriate time for opening the mail but you should be sure of that by challenging the habit and working out the best time. If it is first thing in the morning, all well and good. But if it suits the working arrangements of staff and is no detriment to the company to open the mail at another time, then do so. There are many habit-formed priorities in companies; you should make it a habit always to challenge every routine to make sure that it is being done because that is the right way or time to do it rather than because it is "the way we always do it."

Priorities change

There are basically four reasons why priorities change.

Genuinely

No matter how well time managed and planned you are, no matter how well organized your company is, there will be times when priorities change because of unforeseen circumstances. An airline company, for example, will have a plan of its routine tasks to be dealt with daily, weekly, and monthly, and may successfully work to that plan, but priorities will genuinely change if news is received that one of its aircraft has crashed. Certain departments will have to put aside their routine work to deal with the genuinely changed priority.

In such circumstances, the good time manager absorbs the effect of such crises by reclassifying tasks on the grid of urgency, arranging further delegations where necessary or possible, and planning ahead. Planning ahead might include spending a short time telephoning people who are expecting something from you that is urgent and important and who would not accept excuses easily but who would, if the situation was explained to them, understand why such a circumstance creates a short delay. Never let that be a reason for offering pathetic excuses: always make sure that you do not "cry wolf"; cry "genuine urgent priority change" only when it is so. Be sure that your forward planning involves a rigid reprioritization that will bring your routine tasks back into line as quickly as possible.

Because of lack of planning

Many changes in priorities, even if genuine, could have been foreseen with very little forethought. Many companies are, by their nature, forced to react to their customers or suppliers, and if this is the case, then flexibility should be brought into prioritization to allow for inevitable changes. Thinking ahead can also eliminate that so often heard phrase, "It's obvious when you look at it with hindsight."

"Domino" effect

Your lack of planning or prioritization causes localized chaos that affects other departments in your company. Similarly, lack of planning and prioritization in other departments can affect you. Whether or not, as chaos theory suggests, a butterfly beating its wings over Peking can cause a hurricane in the Caribbean, chaos in one department of the company can almost certainly cause a hurricane in other departments. If you plan and prioritize according to these guidelines, yours will not be the butterfly wings, but you should encourage staff of other departments to consider the same guidelines, if only for your own sake.

As a means of drawing this to their attention, it is worth recording the times when you have been forced to change your priorities because of others and confronting them with that effect, documented if possible.

Panic

It is an unfortunate fact of corporate life that many managers tend to leave everything until the last minute and act as if last minute pressure and crisis was the only incentive to action. As a result, everything they do, and cause to happen around them, is fraught with bad timekeeping, bad prioritization, and ineffective planning. Some managers react to priority changes as if they were the world's greatest disasters. Their lack of perspective about changes causes them to feel threatened, and their response can be summed up by the following:

> *When in danger*
> *when in doubt*
> *run in circles*
> *scream and shout.*

As the secretary to such a manager, you will find that the screaming and shouting is aimed at you and that your boss will solve his time management problems by creating some for you. The problems of boss–secretary prioritization and time management are described below.

Boss–Secretary Priorities

Your boss will tend to see his priorities as much more important than your own. Although it is true to say that your role is supportive of your boss, it should not be forgotten that it is also a role in its own right. If your boss constantly changes your priorities then he must realize that the "domino" effect will be directly on him. Your boss must be encouraged in the boss–secretary partnership to respect your job, to respect your need for and right to prioritization and planning, and to learn to change your priorities for his own purposes only in circumstances of genuine need. Such changes should not arise because of lack of planning, a domino effect that he is passing on to you, or blind panic.

We suggest that, having created your grid of urgency and your priorities, you monitor and record every time your priorities are changed as a result of your boss. Identify those which are genuine, those that arise because of lack of planning, those that are the result of the domino effect, and those that are the result of panic. Confront your boss with this log and insist that he recognizes that he has inappropriately caused you difficulties, which are in turn causing him difficulties. Build a relationship with your boss where you are able to assist him, where appropriate, in building up a grid of urgency and a priority list for him, and assist her in learning this valuable time management technique.

A common example secretaries in our training courses have reported to us is the boss who runs red-faced into your office at 4:55 P.M. demanding that you stay late to get a particular letter ready, which is "desperately urgent." You do so and then on visits to your boss's office during the next three days you see the letter lying on his desk waiting to be sent out. Such an interruption should be challenged and pointed out to your boss, with specific examples of how that improper change of your priorities affected you, and affected your boss.

If your boss is not prepared to enter into a boss–secretary partnership with you regarding priorities and planning, then you will find yourself in a very unsatisfying position. Any sensible boss will listen to your advice but those who will not must face the fact that one day you will improve your environment, get yourself an effective boss–secretary partnership, and manage your time better by the simple expedient of getting a new boss, probably in a new company.

The Time Bandits

During any working day, you will suffer from attacks from the time bandits. Earlier we pointed out that while you might chase, apprehend, and prosecute someone stealing money from you, you are very likely to allow time bandits to steal time from you unchallenged. Over the years of our training with secretaries, the following 15 time bandits have been by far the most commonly reported.

Badly organized and badly run meetings

A deficient meetings culture in your company will affect you as a secretary in many ways. First, if you are minutes secretary to the meeting you will find it difficult to synthesize what is being said for the minutes if a weak chairperson allows rambling discussions with topics being discussed over and over again, does not bring in a broad range of views, and allows loudmouthed people to dominate the meeting. Your time is further wasted by the domino effects of people not turning up and certain sections of the agenda having to be carried forward to other agendas. Other problems include people not reading the minutes you publish and overly extending meetings while they do so. Imagine a room with 20 people spending nearly an hour reading your minutes; you are the one person sitting there drumming your fingers, the one person who can hardly not have read them.

Second, even if you are not minutes secretary to the meeting but the secretary to one of the people in the meeting, if the meeting is not planned with an end time, then you will be constantly interrupted by people trying to find out if your boss is free yet. You will not be able to plan times for your boss to return telephone calls or make appointments inside or outside your company, and so on.

How to arrest the time bandit

A highly effective and highly successful plan for well-organized and well-run meetings that you as secretary can implement with your company is outlined in Volume 1 of *The Professional Secretary's Handbook: Communication Skills*. This training has been delivered by the authors of this book in some of Britain's largest companies, where feedback indicates much more energized meetings and thousands of staff hours saved. We recommend you implement the techniques set out in that volume as soon as possible.

Bad delegation

If you give someone a job and he does it badly, there is a temptation to take it from him and finish it properly yourself. If you do this, then the person you have given it to will know that he can return to you poor quality work without any repercussion on himself. He will solve his time management problems by creating some for you.

How to arrest the time bandit

The way you give tasks to your staff will make a great deal of difference to the commitment they will give to the task. Effective delegation is a skill, (see Delegation beginning on page 75). We recommend that you implement the techniques the next time you are delegating work.

Overcommunication

One of the most common problems in modern companies is not a lack of communication but a surplus of useless information. This arises principally in two ways.

First is a "shotgun" attitude to distribution lists. Quite often when producing a document, either a short memo or a long report, those preparing the document will dream up a long distribution list to make sure they do not miss any important people. This arises from lazy thinking; a little time spent on their part would identify the right people for distribution and eliminate the rest.

Second, overcommunication arises from a lack of synthesis on a writer's part. Imagine you have to convey three facts to another person. You can point to a floor-to-ceiling bookcase and tell her that the three facts are among the 2,000 books there. Alternatively you give her the three facts on one sheet of paper. In both cases, you can be said to have presented her with the facts but in the first case in a useless and time-wasting way, and in the second case in an effective, time-considerate way. Although the example may be an exaggeration there are many times when a two- or three-page report (as it should be) is presented as a 20- or 25-page report full of "nice to know" rather than "need to know" information.

How to arrest the time bandit

If you are involved in writing and creating distribution lists for your boss, then consider that synthesis to the lowest possible level of information flow is your job. Read the section on persuasive writing in Volume 1 of *The Professional Secretary* where principles of editing and synthesis are set out.

Regarding distribution lists, one practical step you should take immediately is to go through every document you receive in your department for yourself and/or your boss and remove either or both of yourselves from distribution lists where you are receiving information you do not want.

Finally, protect your boss from overcommunication by agreeing with her that you can deal with certain matters that do not then have to be passed to the boss, and pass on only those matters that must be dealt with by the boss personally. The secretary who does not synthesize for her own boss is not taking full responsibility for her part in the boss–secretary partnership.

Indecision

You will waste many people's time by being indecisive, and suffer time bandits by other people's indecision. Good decision making in a business environment is a skill with simple rules but one that requires rigid self-discipline. Decisions that are not made but put off until later, decisions that are delayed by obviously false requests for more information, and poorly thought out decisions all create dissatisfaction in your department and in your company. They force further decision making to correct further problems and create a cycle of time wasting. Even in a simple situation, if your staff are waiting for your decision as to whether the cabinets should be put at one end of the room or another, then there will be a great deal of dissatisfaction and loss of respect for you if that decision is not made expediently, sensibly, and forcefully.

How to arrest the time bandit

Consider a six-stage plan for effective decision making:

1. Clarify the situation. Make sure you know what has created the situation and be sure that this is a decision that is yours to take. Clarify deadlines, resources, and objectives. Clarify what further information you might need.

2. Consult with others to make sure that you have all the information necessary. Possibly hold a consultation meeting with those involved in the decision. At that meeting, or during discussions, make clear how you propose to implement the decision and when and what right of appeal is open to those affected by the decision once implemented.

3. Combine all the information gathered together. Plan how you are going to implement the decision.

4. *Make the decision.*
5. Communicate the decision that has been taken, and the effects of that decision. Request feedback from those affected by the decision so that you can monitor its success or ineffectiveness.
6. Check that your decision is being carried out, that it is working successfully and curing the difficulty that it was created to deal with. Review any feedback and if necessary "tweak" the plan, fine-tuning your decision.

These are the five Cs (and one M) of effective decision making. Most importantly, communicate what you are doing so that at times when it may not be obvious to others that you are in your decision-making process, they know that something is happening, and that you are not ignoring the issue.

Open door policy

We recommend an open door policy where your staff are free to approach you to communicate their successes, or problems, and where information flow can be at its most informal. This creates an easy and open working atmosphere, which is good for morale and motivation. However, you need time to yourself when you can plan to deal with certain of your priorities and during that time you should not be interrupted. This goes not just for your staff but for your boss as well. (We look at this in more detail elsewhere.) An open door policy must go hand-in-hand with specific periods of time when your door is closed for your benefit, and this must be respected by all parties.

How to arrest the time bandit
Broadcast loudly times when you do not want to be disturbed and make sure that your staff and your boss respect this. Use those times wisely to deal with your priorities so that you have freed up the maximum time to deal with the everyday running of your department with your staff (see The Workplace, beginning on page 101).

Lack of planned priorities

In this section, we have examined how to prioritize and identify the urgent and the important. If you do not plan your priorities, then you cannot deal with various tasks in an appropriate order.

How to arrest the time bandit
Make sure that you are familiar with the principles of prioritization. Use the "grid of urgency" routinely, and where possible encourage your boss to do the same.

Lack of self-discipline

No matter how well you plan, and no matter how well you know the rules of certain management techniques such as delegation, they are of no value if you do not put them into practice. Very often, we see in training people who are well aware of what they should be doing but who admit that they do something else. For example, they complete their grid of urgency, prioritize tasks to be done in order, and then completely ignore the list and do the tasks they wanted to do anyway. Alternatively, we have heard of people well familiar with the rules of delegation who still insist on delegating tasks that they don't like but should be doing, and retaining for themselves tasks they do enjoy that are completely inappropriate for them to be dealing with.

How to arrest the time bandit

If you lack discipline, then you should challenge your every decision, good or bad, and be sure that it is in line with your knowledge of what should be done. It is sometimes effective to pretend that you are someone else and, when you take an action or make a decision, "talk" to this person (you) and ask yourself to explain to you why you did what you did, or why you have made the decision you have. If this is a persistent problem with you then you can further reinforce this by forcing "the other person" (you) to write down your explanations. Nothing clarifies a situation quite so well as explaining it to "someone else."

Inability to say "no"

In every workplace, there is someone who will try to get you to do his work for him. There are inappropriate requests made, where people are effectively solving their own time management problems by making them yours or, for even lazier people, freeing up time so that they can chat to their friends (wasting their friends' time) while getting you to do their work for them. If you do not say "no" to these inappropriate requests, then you will have to do your own work and other people's during the day and you will end up having to stay late to complete it. Eventually, you will end up being reprimanded by your boss for failing to get all your work done. Few things waste more time than the inability to throw back at people inappropriate demands they are making.

How to arrest the time bandit

The ability to say "no" arises from leaving your nonassertiveness behind and becoming assertive. Practical steps in becoming assertive are explained in the section on assertiveness in Volume 1 of *The Professional Secretary*. We recommend you go through those processes, and make it a principle to challenge inappropriate requests and, assertively, turn them back on the people who are "trying it on."

Unplanned telephone calls out

Certain telephone calls, while they have to be made during a given working day, can be made at any time during that day. If those calls are made *ad hoc* or reactively—whenever you become aware of the situation—then they will be interrupting your flow of dealing with your priorities. Some calls have to be dealt with on that basis, but those that do not can waste a great deal of time if they are made inappropriately.

How to arrest the time bandit

In the section The Workplace (see page 101), we set out rules for dealing with the telephone. Most appropriately, for arresting time bandits, you should plan to make as many telephone calls as possible at a certain time when you are ready to make the calls, when you have the information you need on hand, and when you are in the appropriate place to make the calls (usually your own office). These calls are then dealt with much more efficiently, usually much more quickly, and usually without having to call back later with information you forgot to get ready or to deal with responses you had not anticipated.

Poor handling of paperwork

Despite the onset of the "paperless office," paperwork—and even its electronic form—is a large part of your life as secretary. Poor handling of paperwork can include partially dealing with points, leaving them and then coming back to them time and time again, ignoring urgent matters, inappropriately dealing with nonurgent matters, overcommunicating, failing to deal with the mail quickly, and failing to use the wastepaper basket enthusiastically!

How to arrest the time bandit

In the section Paperwork (beginning on page 96), we give a set of guidelines for dealing with paperwork in an efficient and effective way. This requires the setting of routines, which you should as far as possible rigidly adhere to. Therefore you will need your self-discipline with you at all times.

"Ever-mounting" in-tray

Even if you prioritize effectively and deal with your priorities in an appropriate order, poor time management can lead to the less prioritized items not being dealt with until they become urgent and important. On that basis, your in-tray mounts increasingly toward the ceiling. As well as causing you to fail to get your work done, and possibly to miss appropriate deadlines, an in-tray that is out of control becomes a weight on your shoulders. You cannot concentrate effectively on the work you should be doing because of some vague feeling that you are not in control of your own office.

How to arrest the time bandit

The cure for an ever-mounting in-tray is to dispense with the idea of a single in-tray and to have a collection of trays, each reflecting certain tasks and each being dealt with by certain "diary-based" deadlines. In the section Trays (beginning on page 98), we set out a list of trays you should consider and ways in which they should be dealt with. Combine this with an effective diary, (see page 101), and your in-tray will never grow unnecessarily again.

Personal disorganization

Organization starts immediately when you arrive at work. An analysis of secretarial staff indicated that they could be divided between those who "officially" started their day and those who "fell into it" with a cup of coffee in their hands.

The former group took five to ten minutes at the beginning of the morning, every morning, to make sure that they were familiar with what was in all of their in-trays, that they found out what situations were likely to arise for themselves or their bosses by reviewing both diaries, and that their desks were organized in such a way that they could begin work efficiently. They would check that they had pens, papers, loaded staplers, and so on (and retrieve any from anyone who had borrowed them), that their computers were switched on and open to the appropriate entry screen, and so on.

The latter group picked up a cup of coffee, sat down and either dealt with the first thing that came to mind, or waited until the first demand on them before pushing their chairs forward toward their cluttered and disorganized desks.

For the sake of that ten minutes in the morning, the former group were organized throughout the day; the latter group never seemed to catch up with the day and ended it, flustered and frustrated, just as disorganized as they started it. Of course, this is partly owing to personal style: those who are organized at the beginning of the day probably have the ability to remain organized and those who are disorganized probably lack organization and self-discipline (both cured by reading this book, we hope!). However, it seems that there is some evidence from the descriptions given to us that the former group organized their day in those first few minutes by taking a bird's-eye view of the probable day ahead, so that there were fewer surprises.

How to arrest the time bandit

Make it a rule to spend ten minutes at the beginning of the day organizing your desk and your in-trays and taking that overview of the likely day ahead. Although there are going to be unpredictable situations arising, for most secretaries, most events in most days are predictable. The sun comes up every morning; why let that take you by surprise?

The office chatterer

You will waste a great deal of your time during the day if you are prey to that common time bandit, the chatterer. She will insist on telling you in nauseating detail the events in last night's soap opera on television despite your obvious boredom and lack of interest. When she has finished telling you about that, she will go on to discuss her ailments, her last good vacation, her last three bad vacations, and so on and on and on. The problem is further compounded if the office chatterer happens to be your boss!

How to arrest the time bandit

You will need assertiveness techniques to deal with this person, particularly if it is the boss, and therefore we recommend you read the section on assertiveness in Volume 1 of *The Professional Secretary*.

Specifically, you should make it clear to the person that you have priorities to deal with and deadlines to meet, and you must ask him to respect your rights to get on with your work. If you are happy to talk, then ask him to talk with you at coffee breaks or mealtimes. If you do not want to talk, other than normal everyday bits of conversation, then you should make that clear too. If you use assertiveness techniques, then his initial disappointment should not degenerate into hostility but into a respect for your being a fair person to deal with.

The world is not, of course, ideal and you will not please everyone, but you must have the strength to realize that you are defending your own rights and giving the other person the opportunity to defend his own and join you in that while asking him to respect yours. That is as much as you can or should do; others have responsibilities too.

If the chatterer is your boss, then you must assertively straighten out the situation. Ask to speak to your boss in private, explain that his time management is dependent on your time management and that your need for time to concentrate on tasks is vital for both of you. As before, set aside time for friendly chatting between you when it is convenient to you both. It is important that you both respect the boss–secretary partnership if you are to be a successful and productive team. You must remember that you have the right to mold the world to respecting your rights, providing that you respect the rights of others. If your boss is not prepared to do that, then ultimately you may have to decide to ask for a transfer or even a change of employment. If that sounds extreme, remember the analogy of the money bandit stealing your purse and how angry you would be; remember that you should by now have learned to value time at least as importantly as you value money. You will be spending a large chunk of your lifetime in your work environment, which must therefore work for you.

In various of our secretarial training courses, and in secretarial conferences we have addressed, we have had lighthearted competitions for the most radical solution to the office chatterer (the prize was a set of false teeth!). The two suggestions that got the loudest applause follow. We are not especially recommending them, but what they lack in assertiveness they make up for in originality.

The first is what was called the "Howard Hughes touch." Apparently the reclusive billionaire, whenever he did not want to hear someone, simply cocked his head to one side with his finger pushing on his earlobe and asked the person to repeat what she had said. He would continue doing this endlessly until the person finally gave up. Eventually all his staff (by which we mean those privileged to deal with him personally) came to know that as soon as he made that gesture, they should immediately not waste their time and they would back away from the situation, apparently to his satisfaction. He had programmed them with a key gesture that told them that from that point they were totally wasting their time and they made their own decision about how to deal with that, which was the decision he had intended them to make.

The second most appreciated suggestion was that you should bone up on a totally absurd subject to the point where you could discuss it with great conviction.

Suggestions offered were in the order of a firm belief in fairies, for example. Whenever pushed into conversation, you would turn that conversation around to your chosen subject and totally bore the office chatterer with excruciating detail about this absurd subject, about which (you hope) she had no interest whatsoever (if she turned out to be interested, you would have to find something even more boring to talk about).

We stress again that we are not recommending these techniques, but we should point out that those who suggested them claimed they work very well!

Being drawn into other people's problems

Something like the office chatterer are people who insist on you being drawn into their difficulties, at home, with the boss, with their job, and so on. They use you as a sounding board to tell you how bad their sister's boyfriend is, how inefficient the boss is, and why their new car is not all they expected it would be.

How to arrest the time bandit

Assertiveness is again the key to dealing with people like this and all the points mentioned above can be used in these situations. You also have the right to point out that these are not problems that affect you, and that although you are happy to discuss mutually interesting things, you do not want to discuss something you have no involvement with and can gain no personal benefits from.

You might also turn the problem back on the person, who almost certainly is not looking for suggestions so much as someone to moan at, by making suggestions. If he is complaining that his car is not all it should be, suggest that the proper course of action is to take it to a garage and get a diagnosis, and tell him that on the basis of the diagnosis you would be prepared to discuss specific points raised. Almost certainly he will get the message that you are being business-like, which reinforces your other statements that you have business to deal with.

You must know from the outset, in the cases of the office chatterer and those drawing you into their problems, that you have the right not to be drawn into other people's situations if you do not want to. Those people who feign to be, or who genuinely are, upset by your lack of interest are manipulating you to be part of their world on their terms against your wishes. You do not have to buy friendships, at work or elsewhere, and your true friends or valued colleagues are those who will respect you standing up for yourself and being a fair person to deal with.

Other people's lack of concern for you

In one sense, this is a summary of all the points above, but there are many other, perhaps less specific, areas where people exhibit a lack of concern for you.

How to arrest the time bandit

First, you must be assertive in dealing with such people and make sure that they understand that you expect your rights to be respected.

Second, you must examine these random situations and make sure that you are acting appropriately. When you have made a decision, implement it.

Third, as an experiment that will aid in your own assertiveness development, make a list right now of five irritating things in your office where people appear to be exhibiting a lack of concern for you (other than the points above). Then make sure that you list ways in which you will deal with those problems and begin to implement them by—at the latest—the end of the month in which you are reading this book.

Exercise 1

You could do some useful team building in your department by instigating a brainstorm among all the people there to identify and list the ten worst time bandits in your department and agree on radical solutions for arresting them.

Delegation

Delegation is not just the handing down of work to subordinates or others. If tasks naturally fall to other people, then your job as a manager is simply to make sure that they are well briefed and that they know the job is theirs to deal with. Theirs is the responsibility for the job and they are accountable for its outcome.

Delegation is something quite different. Delegation is the giving of a job to someone else that you, as a secretarial team leader or secretarial department manager, might have otherwise decided to do yourself, or which might have been appropriate for you to do. In this way, delegation is the allocation of authority and responsibility to others while you retain the overall accountability for the actions or decisions.

Exercise 2

Do you need to delegate more?

	Yes	No

Do you lack confidence in the abilities and experience of your staff?

Are you afraid to take risks?

Are you concerned that poor decision making by others will rebound on you?

Have you been described as too perfectionist?

Do you spend too much time looking at details and less time looking at the overall planning and functions of your department?

Do you have difficulty meeting deadlines?

Do you have unfinished jobs accumulating on your desk?

Do you have a pile of jobs accumulating on your desk that have been done by your subordinates and that you have insisted on reviewing, but for which you have not found the time?

	Yes	No

Do you constantly monitor the progress of jobs you have delegated
   instead of letting your subordinates get on with the work?

Are your standards so high that you feel only you can achieve them?

Do you take work home on a regular basis either in the evenings or on
   weekends?

Do you work longer hours than your subordinates?

Do you find yourself doing tasks your subordinates ought to be doing?

Are you often interrupted by your subordinates with questions, requests,
   advice, demands for decisions, permission to go ahead?

The more times you have checked "yes," the more you need to delegate. The more "yes" boxes there are, the less you are "letting go of the reins" of jobs and the less you are trusting your staff. This is bad for you and bad for them. Consider the following advice very carefully and make a decision that you will delegate more, starting immediately, using the guidelines given.

Why we do not like delegating

A great deal of research has gone into finding out why people avoid delegation. The main reasons are as follows.

It is risky

Many people believe that by delegating jobs to others, they are risking reprisals if the job is not done well or if the outcomes are not as expected.

Observation. Delegation *is* risky, but the most enlightened companies now realize that their greatest advances come from risk taking, whereas caution breeds stagnation. That is not to say that risk taking should be equated with recklessness, and there are guidelines that make delegation effective (see page 81). As a manager, you should make sure that you work within a culture of sensible risk taking.

We enjoy doing the tasks ourselves

Many people do not delegate jobs that they are enjoying, or jobs that have a high profile (the ones that get a pat on the back from the boss).

Observation. By delegating to others jobs that get a pat on the back from the boss you can motivate others while freeing further time for possibly higher priority work. You should not be doing easy things; you should be doing effective things.

No time to think and plan

People avoid delegation on the grounds that it takes time to work out who to delegate to and how to do it; and that time is not available.

Observation. This is often true but only because you have failed to think out the full length of time needed to deal with the task. If you start thinking about a task when the deadlines are almost on top of you, then you will be in crisis management; by proper planning, you will have time to deal with the delegation issue, which in the long term will be good time management for you.

It is too slow
Many people argue that delegation is pointless because "it's quicker to do it myself."

Observation. On a one-time-only basis, this may be true. On the other hand, if you invest time now in delegating a task to a subordinate who can deal with it in the future, then from your time management point of view in the long term, you will spend a good deal less time doing the task, as it will not be coming around again in later months or years. One of the Third World support charities had a very effective slogan: "If you give a man a fish, you feed him for a day; if you teach a man to fish, you feed him for life." Stop giving your staff fish, and start teaching them how to fish.

We like to keep on top of everything
People avoid delegation because they feel they will lose touch with tasks that they have some affinity to.

Observation. Your head is only a certain size and you can only contain within it a certain number of things; the day is just so long and you only have a limited number of eyes, arms, and legs. Failing to delegate means that you are stagnant, in that you are not releasing tasks to others that enable you to take on new tasks and develop yourself. When you seriously argue that you will not delegate because "you like to keep on top of everything," you are telling your bosses, "I have reached the limits of my abilities." Do you really want to tell them that?

Our subordinates may turn out to be better at tasks than we are
People avoid delegation because of the possible embarrassment of discovering that they have not been doing a job well and that their subordinates can do it better.

Observation. We hope this will turn out to be true. Rather than castigating yourself for not doing a job well, you might compliment yourself for being a better manager than a doer, i.e., you may not have been able to do the task but you were able to delegate it effectively, having found the right person and given her the right briefing. The fact that your subordinates can do tasks better than you can is a compliment to your managerial skills and a foot on the promotional ladder. The chairperson of your company cannot possibly have done every task that ever had to be done in your company but she is chairperson because, to quote the advertisement, she "knows someone who can."

If you want a job done properly, do it yourself
Many people avoid delegation because they feel that only they are capable of attaining the standards they demand and do not trust that others can.

Observation. If this is true, then it reflects on your own bad delegation abilities. You need to read this section urgently. In fact, this is usually just a pathetic excuse for not wanting to admit to one of the six other reasons above.

Alternatives to delegation

Alternatives to delegation fall into good and bad categories, particularly when viewed from the point of view of time management. Throughout these examples, we will use the following situation. You have typed a 30-page report. You have decided that Jane, your subordinate, will do the job of preparing 30 copies of the report and distributing them.

Bad alternatives to delegation include instruction and abdication.

Instruction

Instruction is where you give the task to someone else but demand that she constantly checks up with you at each stage before moving on to the next stage. You are constantly looking over her shoulder and insisting that she does the task in a way that you approve of.

In the situation above, you would ask Jane to take your master copy to the photocopier, tell her to make 30 copies and then to come back to you for further instruction. When she comes back to you, you then tell her to bind them into 30 bound copies and then come back to you for further instruction. When she comes back to you with 30 bound copies, you then give her the distribution list and ask her to prepare 30 covering letters and come back to you for further instruction. When she comes back to you with 30 bound copies and 30 letters, you then tell her to put a letter with each bound copy, put them in the envelopes, address all the envelopes, and bring them back to you so that you can inspect them before asking her to take them down to the mailroom.

It is highly demotivating to be treated like a tame monkey or a robot. No matter how successful Jane is in making good quality photocopies, making sure that they are well collated, and that the envelopes contain accurate packages and accurate addresses and are distributed on time, she will never feel that the job was hers. The credit will always, at least in her mind, go to you. She will feel used rather than motivated. She has added nothing of herself to the job and lacks job satisfaction.

Furthermore, the best possible outcome of instruction is that the job will be done to the same standards as your own. You might regard that as good, but many in your company might regard an improvement over your standards as highly desirable! Instruction does not allow Jane to improve on your abilities.

Abdication

If delegation is, as we have stated above, the allocation of authority and responsibility, but not overall accountability, to subordinates, then abdication is the dismissal of all authority and responsibility to subordinates along with an attempt to unload the accountability for failure. It could be summed up as: do it any way you want but don't come back to me, don't ask me for help, and don't blame me if it all goes wrong.

In our situation, you would give the master copy of the report to Jane, tell her that you want 30 copies of the report to be in the mail tonight to 30 given names and addresses, and tell her you don't want to see her again. If she has any difficulties, if she finds the photocopier is broken down, if she finds the addresses are incomplete, or she knows they are inaccurate, you do not want her to come back for advice or help. You are trying to create a denial of your own accountabilities. It may be the making of Jane to throw her into the deep end of the swimming pool in order to discover if she can learn how to swim. She might, but it is hardly constructive to throw her off a moving ship in the middle of the Pacific Ocean!

Without the support of her boss (you), Jane will feel that if mistakes are made, it will be on her head, whereas if she is successful, there will be no praise and, possibly, you will be taking any credit for yourself. This is demotivating and unsatisfying. Furthermore, Jane will never have the opportunity to find out if her approach was better or worse than yours would have been and she may create an even worse way of doing the task, which will then become "department standard." This lowers the efficiency of the department when, with a little constructive assistance from yourself, it could have been raised.

Good alternatives to delegation include support and swapping.

Support

Many companies are demonstrating that delegation, whether it is to subordinates or laterally to colleagues, or even back to bosses, is not the only positive way of dealing with tasks. Delegation could be somewhat loosely summed up as: "Who can I give this task to?" If this is so, then support could equally be summed up as: "Who can help me with this task?"

Support suggests that within our departments, we should be looking around for the most appropriate or the most skilled person for individual tasks and asking her to assist in raising standards. This of course only works in a situation where those people can similarly ask for support from you. Support leads to swapping.

Swapping

Swapping could be summed up as: "What can they do for me, and what can I do for them?" Many small, radical companies (typically computer software development companies) are looking at systems of swapping tasks rather than delegating them, where time management problems are eased by having people trained in a multifaceted way. At times of heavy requirements in one particular area there are other people who can join in and deal with the tasks.

This is not much different than what has been going on in companies for many years, with other people "filling in." The main difference is the difference between the words "trained" and "filling in." By anticipation of a need for swapping, and the setting up of a culture of swapping, appropriate training can be given to broaden people's abilities so that standards do not drop at times of crisis.

Why delegate?

There are three well-known reasons for delegating. However, there is a fourth one that you must be aware of and in agreement with, because otherwise you will not delegate effectively or honestly.

The three well-known reasons are:

- it spreads the workload;
- it makes time available;
- it allows you time and scope to develop new abilities.

Delegation is a time management technique designed to make sure that you are using your time most effectively and applying tasks to others in a way that leaves you free to do the tasks you should be doing. This cannot be the whole picture, however. The fourth and lesser recognized reason for delegation is:

- delegation develops and trains others.

We must recognize that we should be giving people tasks because those tasks, whether or not it is appropriate for us to do them, are also necessary for their personal development and training. This is a long-term benefit to the department, the company as a whole, and the individual to whom you are delegating. If you do not recognize this as a reason for delegation, then you are only delegating to help yourself and not others. This is dishonest and inappropriate. You will delegate the wrong tasks to the wrong people and with the wrong attitude; standards in your department will fall. Recognition of the importance of developing and training others is one of the most important qualities of a good manager and one that you should seek to develop if you are seeking promotion within the secretarial ranks.

What tasks should you delegate?

The simple answer is: every type of task.

Tasks you can do less well than others

The fact that you do them less well than others is not a reason for delegation but it could be that you are doing them less well because you know that it is inappropriate that you should be doing them. You should have the courage to release them to others who may find them motivating and who can develop them better than you can.

Tasks you do not like doing

Again the fact that you do not like doing tasks is not a reason for delegation, but you should not be afraid to delegate tasks that you do not like doing. For one thing, those tasks may be necessary for the development and training of others; second, you should not be afraid to make important management decisions and give people tasks that—while they may not like them—they either need to do or have a duty to do.

Although we would not suggest, as General Patton is held to have said, that "I measure the weakness of an officer by every man under his command who likes him," we recognize that management is not a friendship contest. Others have responsibilities and a good manager makes them clear.

Tasks you love doing

As before, the fact that you love doing tasks is not a reason for delegating them, but you should realize that sometimes you cling to tasks you should not be doing because you have grown out of them. Those tasks may well be needed to develop and train others and you should be prepared to release them. Furthermore, they may be highly enjoyable tasks and by sharing them, you will not only motivate others but will show that you are a fair leader and not just trying to give yourself an easy ride at the expense of others.

Tasks needed to develop others

Any task that will develop and train your staff to the benefit of your department, your company, and themselves should be delegated effectively. This is the all-embracing category.

High-profile tasks

All of us have a natural tendency to cling to high-profile tasks that give us a round of applause. Remember that if they are motivating for us, they are motivating for our subordinates, and we can generate a highly motivated team by sharing the high-profile tasks appropriately.

For example, if you have traditionally prepared and organized a conference for 100 of your sales force at a prominent conference location, and if at the end of the conference your chairperson calls you up on the stage to take a round of applause, be sure that you are prepared to allow someone else that pleasure in the future. If you determine that you should delegate that task to your subordinate, remember to allow him to take the applause on stage next time and do not go up yourself, even as department head. The former is highly motivating and will encourage people to seek to do that task (and relieve the time pressure from you) in the future. The latter approach would demotivate your staff, getting yourself a name as an egotist, and ensuring that you will have difficulty in delegating the task in the future.

Guidelines for effective delegation

Consider applying, immediately, the following guidelines for the next tasks you delegate.

Decide what tasks to delegate and to whom they should be delegated

Bear in mind that the selection of tasks and staff depends on the overall effectiveness of your department and on tasks needed to develop others as well as to free up time for yourself.

Determine what training may be needed for the task

Consult with the member of staff concerned and arrange appropriate training prior to handing over the task and, if necessary, maintenance training during longer projects.

Define the responsibility, reasons, and objectives of the task

Do this by inspiring your member of staff with a vision that shows how her completion of the task plays an important part in the work of your department.

Determine any limitations that may have to be imposed, such as budgetary limitations, deadlines, and so on.

Determine and communicate the level of authority

Make clear what actions can and cannot be taken without further consultation with you.

Agree on target times for completion, or stages of completion

You cannot impose a target time; this must be done by agreement with the staff member. If you demand that the task is completed by a certain time and it is not, then your subordinate can argue that the failure to meet the deadline is yours for setting an impractical deadline rather than his own. He may argue that he always knew it could not be done but that he tried to meet your requirements. If you agree on target times for either the completion of a task or stages of completion in consultation, then the subordinate "owns" the deadline and will try harder to meet it.

Ask when a task can be completed; get an estimate from the subordinate but be ready to negotiate. There will be a tendency on your subordinate's part to pad out the estimate to give himself buffer time, but this will serve only to slow him down; an effective target should be realistic but difficult. Negotiate such a target to keep your staff alert and energized.

Agree with your subordinate on times when you expect feedback or follow-up

Determine the reporting procedures (do you want a written report, a verbal presentation?). You cannot impose this on your subordinate; you must negotiate with her on a time and a style for this feedback that you both feel will communicate the proper information in the most effective way.

Motivation techniques applied to delegation

Let people "own" the task

Earlier we described the difference between delegation and instruction. With instruction, the person to whom you have given the task does not own the task; she plays no part in its planning, she does not design its implementation, and she gets none of the credit for its success. For the highest levels of motivation when you are delegating, make sure that your subordinates know that the task is theirs, and that its success or failure will reflect on them.

Let people add something of themselves to the task

We would go one step further and suggest that, rather than just letting people add something of themselves to the task, you should encourage people to do so. Whatever the task, however simple or complex, draw out of your subordinates a suggestion for how they would approach some aspect of the task, or what suggestions they might have for alternative ways to deal with certain aspects.

This is also a very useful technique for encouraging reticent or insecure subordinates. You can fix matters so that they seem to have invented something that is fairly normal procedure. The encouragement and motivation that their involvement creates within them will inspire them.

Praise risk taking; do not punish failure

All companies have learned that the way to progress is to build on mistakes. What we learn from success is that we can copy the pattern and have more of the same success. But what we learn from failure is that we can improve the pattern and create greater successes. If you punish failure, then people will not feel confident to try new approaches to problems, they will become overcautious and the best position you will obtain is to maintain the status quo. If you praise risk taking, even if it doesn't work, then you will encourage your staff to try new things and find new successes.

This does not mean that there are not appropriate times for criticism. The proper time for punishment, or at least admonishment, is when people do not learn from their mistakes. Praise them for taking risks even if they fail, and analyze the failures with them so that you can both determine what went wrong and how to put it right. Only criticize anyone who ignores those lessons and continues to make mistakes. Make sure that, even in those circumstances, any criticism given is constructive (see below).

Encourage creativity, not conformity

People who follow the rule book will, at best, only produce the same that has always been produced. Those whose creativity is encouraged will create new ideas, and new products.

This does not mean that total anarchy should reign in your company; there are perfectly good reasons for many rules, not least health and safety, and these cannot be ignored. However, praise the person who challenges every rule, no matter how sensible the rule may seem; praise them again when they find a better way to do things, and praise them even more when they come to the conclusion that the rule is a good one and should be obeyed. Those who have fought through rules and understood them are far more likely to keep to them than those who stick to the rule book without understanding why.

One secretary told us of an experience that had unsettled her on her first week in employment. With the usual limited experience that inevitably follows coming straight from school or college, she had been employed in an office with word processors. She was told not to turn them off, that this task would be done by her supervisor. One evening during her first week, she realized that the supervisor was not there (and she had not been told that there was a backup to deal with it), and thinking that it would be wrong not to turn the computers off when she left, she took the risk and did so. Unfortunately, the system, a rather primitive one by today's standards, shut down in such a way that everyone in the building lost their whole day's computer processing. She remembered being heavily criticized, yet we felt that was hardly fair. Faced with the situation, she had taken a risk based on the information she had on hand; had she had the reasons for not turning the computer off explained to her, she would have had a better understanding. We felt that it was primarily the responsibility of her supervisor not just to tell her the rules, but also to explain the background to them.

Praise effective work, not busy work

We saw a situation in an office that demonstrated to us the value of this rule. Although this did not happen in a secretarial environment, the situation is exactly the same. The department manager was sitting at a clear desk leaning back in his chair with his hand clasped behind his head and his eyes closed. It is worth pointing out that we knew this manager to be highly effective, able to motivate his staff well and lead a well-disciplined and well-organized, productive department. We might go on to add that the company recognized this in due course with significant promotions. At this time, however, his immediate boss came in and asked him what he was doing. "I'm thinking," replied the manager. "You can just as well think at home," was the reply. "You're paid to come here and work, not think." We were quite confident that he would have been thinking through a work-related problem we had all been discussing earlier, and that 15 minutes of his thinking time could save hours, even days, of nonproductive effort on the part of his staff. Yet his manager was the sort who thought that if he was not sweating, scribbling, or otherwise doing something, he wasn't working.

In our own offices we have always adopted the principle of communicating goals, i.e., what tasks need to be achieved and by when, and leaving it to our staff to determine how and when to deal with them. We judge good work as quality work, i.e., meeting the goals and producing effective, productive output. We do not judge good work as seeing the staff busy all the time regardless of the quality of the output. Indeed, in our own company, if staff feel they need a break, then they are free to leave their desks, relax a while, do a bit of shopping, or do whatever else they need to do when they need to do it. If anyone were to take liberties with that freedom, then we are sure that peer pressure from highly motivated and committed colleagues would prevent them taking liberties for long. If they did not meet their goals, then we would know something was adrift. As long as they are continuing to meet their goals and we feel that they are realistically set, then we believe we are getting good work. It is our belief that we will get a higher quality of work, and have more motivated staff, if they work well when they are at their desks rather than if we chain them to their desks for longer hours.

You as the head of your secretarial team should try to operate within this framework, using your motivational skills to get from your staff quality rather than quantity of effort.

Make good work visible

Too often in business we criticize the problems, or at least comment on them, while ignoring successes. We act as if "we pay you for success so you don't need to be praised for it." It is highly motivational to point out good work people have done, not just to them so that they know you have appreciated it, but also to their colleagues so that their good work for the whole department is recognized by everyone affected by it.

Give your praise visibly, in the general office rather than behind your own closed door. This is not to suggest that you should embarrass people by praising too much too publicly, but you can be sure that praise given in a one-to-one conversation at a normal volume of speech will soon get around the grapevine!

Give rewards if they are due

If you have promised a reward for a particular task, perhaps a day off for doing some exceptional overtime, some pay increase, or some other reward, never forget to give the reward. If you make a promise and do not keep it, it is highly demotivating and you will have great difficulty getting the person to offer the same effort the next time.

By the same token, you should not bribe people into doing work. If you have to pay someone extra money to do what is a regular part of his work, then, rather in the manner of a drug addict needing bigger "fixes," the reward becomes a "basic" due to the person and you will have to keep increasing the bribe to get him to do the same level of work.

One secretary told us of a situation where she had been deadlocked by her company, which refused to allow her to give any sort of reward although it was asking her to get her staff constantly to increase their unpaid overtime efforts. She did not promise rewards, but having achieved the goal she had set she bought all her staff boxes of chocolates as a thank-you. She mentioned this to her boss but did not ask him to underwrite the payment, which was from her own pocket. The following day, the boss checked how much she had spent, and gave her the sum from petty cash in an envelope attached to a box of chocolates to her from him. He admitted he had learned the value of appreciating effort and rewarding it.

Say "thank-you"

Two words that are frequently missing from communication in work are the words "thank-you." As stated above, you should think in terms of a response to good work as well as a response to poor work.

Major tasks

There are certain major tasks that can overwhelm your subordinates if presented to them badly—tasks that can seem overwhelming to subordinates because of their sheer scope. Therefore, we suggest that you consider the following guidelines for major tasks.

The stages of progress are not visible

Some tasks are of such long duration (say a five-year project) or of such breadth (organizing a conference for 1,000 people in a year's time) that it is often difficult to know that you are making progress. Confucius said that on a journey of 1,000 miles there has to be a first step, but he failed to point out that after taking a first step you don't feel that you have gone very far.

You don't know where to start

The problem with overwhelming tasks or very complex and long tasks is that it is very difficult to know where to begin. So many different factors can affect so many others that it is easy to begin at the wrong place and waste a lot of time before you realize that you have missed important areas.

You cannot see the whole picture

Unless the task is given to you in an effective way, then you cannot see the overall purpose of the task or goal of the task.

As a result of this, these overwhelming tasks are often ignored or put off on the basis that they can always be started later rather than now (if you are dealing with something that isn't going to happen for a year, then tomorrow looks very much like today). The result is to end up putting it off for six months and rushing the job at the very end as the deadlines become ominously close. Examples of overwhelming tasks are:

- organizing the relocation of your offices to a new building;
- writing a manual for new staff coming into your department or company;
- designing a new layout or uses for the staff cafeteria/rest room;
- organizing a conference for 1,000 people.

How to tackle overwhelming tasks

Don't avoid them

Overwhelming tasks have to be dealt with, and avoiding them will simply make the deadlines all the tighter and the possibility of failure all the more real.

Don't leave them to a New Year's resolution or similar agenda

Rather like giving up smoking or going on a diet, it is always possible to start an overwhelming task tomorrow rather than today for some apparently logical reason. The thinking process goes as follows. "It's now Wednesday and I really ought to have a clear start to this task so I'll put it off until next Monday. But now it's Monday and I've got the weekend's mail and Monday's mail to deal with and that will take me most of the day, so I had better start the task on Tuesday. It's now Tuesday and I can start the task by organizing what's going to have to be done tomorrow, leaving me clear to finish the tasks I know I have to do today. It's now Wednesday . . ."

If the appropriate time to start a task is now, then start it now. In fact, as a guideline a good time to start an overwhelming task is at about three o'clock on a Friday afternoon. This seems to be the least likely time, because you are just about to leave work but the advantage is twofold. First, you will have the weekend for your subconscious to work on the task that you have begun. When you come back to it on

Monday, you will come back refreshed and with some creative ideas for approaching the task. Second, by starting it at the end of Friday and not getting very far, you will have a starting point from which to continue first thing on Monday morning, which will get you into the task more quickly than if you have to start cold first thing on Monday morning.

Divide tasks into bite-sized pieces

Dividing tasks will allow you to see the whole picture more clearly and to monitor stages of progress as each of the pieces is dealt with.

Schedule the work

Make sure that you have the various pieces of the work listed in your grid of urgency and your schedule of priorities, including your longer-term priorities for the year ahead.

Keep going

Make sure that you keep to your schedule and that you treat each target as seriously as any other. The fact that you have a long time for completion is an illusion; the deadlines are still real and they will arrive eventually. If you have ever parachuted out of an aircraft, you will know that the ground seems to remain a long way away until that point when suddenly it rushes up and you are there. Deadlines work a bit like that too.

Promise and give rewards

Whether to yourself or your subordinates, make sure that you make appropriate promises of reward and deliver them in order to keep people motivated. These can be as little as a thank-you or a day off for dealing with particularly pressured tasks.

Make successes visible

At each stage of the implementation of the tasks, make sure that people know that you are aware of their progress. Praise them for the good work done and work constructively with them to correct problems. By the same token, you should not impose yourself too much in work you have delegated to them; let them come to you at agreed feedback times.

Bathe in the "feel good" factor

Let people feel good about the work they have done and, as we suggested earlier, if you give them the task of preparing a conference, make sure that it is they, and not you, who go up on stage and take the applause of the delegates for a good organizational job well done.

When giving a task of this nature to subordinates, the rules are no different from the rules for asking them to do any task. Set their boundaries of authority; make sure that they know their limitations, such as financial budgets, deadlines, and so on, and leave them free to deal with the task within as wide a set of boundaries as possible. In the case of overwhelming tasks, make sure that you communicate the vision to them of the end product. If you are giving them the task of organizing a conference for 1,000 people, then describe to them how you visualize that conference looking:

whether it is glitzy or professional, what kinds of presentations might be made, and what kinds of seating might be available (describe it in a way that still leaves latitude for creativity on the subordinates' part).

Make sure that you have planned between you times for feedback. Monitor the progress of the work. Leave your subordinates to work out how to do it but be sure that they know that you are not abdicating the job, that you are there to give them support when they feel lost. If you have done the task before, let them know so that they can call on you for advice when they are unsure.

This approach will make sure that when the task is completed, they will feel that they owned it and that the successes arising from it are theirs. This is a highly motivational approach and you will make sure that next time the job comes around they will be lining up at your desk to take it away from you rather than running away from you trying to find them. Apart from being good for them, it is excellent time management from your point of view to have people trying to take work away from you!

Summary

A simple summary of the way of motivating others when delegating tasks to them is contained in the phrase:

What gets recognized, gets done.

The Boss–Secretary Partnership

Secretaries' time management issues are more complex than the issues of most managers. The secretary is managing not only her own time but also that of her boss. Effective secretaries must build partnerships with their bosses.

Know your boss

If you are to understand what makes your boss "tick," then you must take the time and trouble to know a good deal about her. There are boundaries that you should not cross—too much involvement in your boss's personal relationships, for example—but you need to be "inside your boss's head" to some degree, understanding her likes and dislikes, preferences, strengths and weaknesses, and so on. This is a good time to remind you that the word *secretary* is based on the word *secret*; that the origin of the word relates to "the keeper of secrets." Part of the partnership is to keep much of what you learn, or come to understand, confidential.

What does your boss want from life?

What tangible needs does your boss have? Does he require more money, a bigger house, flashy cars: the trappings of wealth. In fact, for many people, the assumption of tangible needs is incorrect; the driving forces behind many bosses are usually the less tangible needs. These intangibles include recognition, status, job security, the maximum freedom to make decisions, success, a happy marriage or family life, and so on.

What does your boss want from work?

Your boss's personal objectives are likely to be greatly similar to the intangible needs in life: personal growth, a sense of achievement, recognition by others, job security, the opportunity to become "the person she knows she is capable of becoming." Your boss will also have organizational objectives to be met: target profit and long-term expansion, for example.

What does your boss want from you?

Most bosses' needs include assistance, cooperation, information, dependability, and honesty. Most bosses will tell you that the best secretary they ever had was the one who gave them solutions rather than problems, the one who dealt with things without having to be asked and, indeed, without the boss even knowing that the problem had arisen and been dealt with. "She takes a load off my shoulders" is the boss's evening prayer of thanks to the corporate gods.

What are your boss's strengths and weaknesses?

You must analyze your boss's strengths and weaknesses so that you can help where she needs help most. Learn also to depend on your boss in those areas where she is strongest. Ask yourself questions like: "Is my boss better with dealing with tasks or with people?" "Are my boss's communication and interactive skills good or bad?" "Does my boss manage time well?; is my boss cool in a crisis or panic?" "Does my boss meet deadlines?" "Does my boss set effective deadlines for others?" "Does my boss monitor others well, not too intrusively, and not too uninterestedly?"

What are your boss's likes and dislikes?

Talk to your boss and discuss how he likes to receive information and suggestions: on paper or verbally, at the end of the day or at the beginning of the day, talking over coffee, at the secretary's desk, or at his own desk. Does your boss like to take time to think things over or does he like to talk it over with you, using you as a sounding board for thinking processes? Is your boss tolerant of interruptions? Discuss with him when you can interrupt and when you should not. Is your boss happy for you to make appointments on his behalf or do all appointments have to be checked at the time of making? Make sure your boss is one who prefers solutions rather than problems; most are, but a few might find it presumptuous—present information to your boss in the way he wants to receive it.

Understand your boss's management style

Is your boss more concerned with the rules than with getting things done? Does she operate in a very formal way or on the basis of intuition. Does your boss rely on you or regard you as a robot to do what she requests? Is your boss highly involved in every task or effective at delegating work? Is your boss aggressive, assertive, or nonassertive? Is your boss autocratic or democratic?

Know yourself

If you are to form 50 percent of this boss–secretary partnership, you must not only know your boss, you must know yourself. You should ask yourself all the same questions that you have asked about your boss in terms of what you want from life and from your work, what your strengths and weaknesses are, your likes and dislikes, and your preferred working style.

There are one or two other questions you might consider to be specific to your part of the partnership. For example, are you the sort of person who prefers to be instructed (i.e., given tasks bit by bit with little latitude for personal thought) or are you the sort of person who likes to be given an objective and the freedom and independence to work out the task for yourself? Are you seeking opportunities to learn in this position so that you can be promoted within the secretarial hierarchy or leave the secretarial hierarchy and move into management? What resources have you been offered and what resources do you believe you should have to do your job effectively? Do you expect the relationship to be one of fairness, cooperation, open communication, and consideration for your views?

Synergy at work

An effective team is more than the sum of its parts. Synergy describes that wonderful phenomenon in the most open and empowered teams where one plus one actually does make three. Your relationship with your boss should be one of sharing strengths and removing sources of conflict between yourself and within your department and your company. Start by understanding the "know your boss/know yourself" questions and formalize this by asking your boss what he expects of you. Seek the opportunity to tell your boss what you expect of him.

Write out your own job description as you see it and ask your boss to write out your job description as he sees it. Go further than the formal job description that would be in your personnel file to include all the aspects of "know your boss/know yourself." Go through the two documents together, comparing where you agree with each other and discussing where you disagree. Discuss with your boss his views on effective management styles and approaches and seek the opportunity to influence your boss with your own views. Make sure that the objectives of the partnership are in line with the individual objectives of your boss and yourself. Encourage your boss to make department plans with you; point out to him that you are probably more in touch with the day-to-day desires, needs, complaints, and feelings of the department staff than he is.

Throughout all relationships of this nature, you should try to remain open and flexible, intuitive and creative. Try to encourage this in your boss by leading by example. Remember that bosses get to be bosses because of a number of talents and abilities, not one of which has ever been listed as "the ability to get along with a secretary." It is in your best interest to teach your boss how to manage his secretary (you).

The partnership in practice

The office work for which you as secretary are responsible must be agreed with your boss so that his involvement suits you both.

Typing

It will be your job to type your boss's letters. If you are an executive secretary or administrative assistant, then it may be a task you can delegate to one of your team, but the accountability remains with you. Discuss with your boss how material for typing should be delivered, e.g., taking live dictation in his office on a notepad, taking tapes he has dictated on a dictation machine, taking typing from longhand, or finalizing on your word processor a rough draft that he has typed into his word processor. All of these are now common and there will be times when, driven by circumstances, you will have to deal with all four types of delivery. However, you should discuss with your boss a preferred method of delivery for the bulk of material.

Consider the following points for discussion. First, live dictation is a time bandit compared to a dictation machine. With a dictation machine, your boss can dictate on his own and then pass you the tape, which you transcribe. With live dictation, the two of you have to be together during the dictation, but there is no saving for you in transcription. From the boss's point of view he can also break off from dictation for interruptions such as telephone calls without wasting your time. If your boss wants to get the most out of your available time, then he should obtain, and learn to use, a dictation machine as soon as possible. Second, typing from longhand is time consuming and usually ineffective. For one thing, most bosses seem to acquire almost indecipherable hieroglyphics the more senior they become, and you will not be able to read their handwriting anyway. Furthermore, it is a time consuming method of drafting. Your boss would be well advised to learn how to use a word processor for those occasional letters or long reports where he wishes to do the first draft. This is not impractical; sometimes your boss will need to formulate his own ideas before giving them to you to finalize, or prepare copies for distribution. He can do that more effectively through a word processor than in handwritten draft form, the word processor being a much more flexible instrument for initial drafting. However, it has to be said that many bosses have never learned to type and those individuals are hardly likely to at this stage in their careers. Take comfort from the fact that bosses now moving up the ladder are usually highly computer literate and in some cases can type as quickly as you can. Restrict typing from handwritten drafts to those occasions when your boss drafts a document on the train, at home in front of the TV, or somewhere where he might be using his time well to do the drafting but where he has no access to a word processor.

Filing and general office management

The majority of your boss's filing should be under your administration. Therefore, your boss should allow you to set up filing and office systems that suit you rather than him. You will be doing the filing, you will be retrieving filing, and you will be dealing with other department staff in maintaining the general systems of the office.

Therefore, the motivating and effective way for you to deal with that is to have some considerable part in the designing of those processes. There are, however, a few points to be considered. First, your filing may have to follow a pattern of filing elsewhere in the company in order to standardize systems that may make overall training and transferability of staff more efficient. Second, there may be good reasons for the existing system even if it is unique, and you should take the trouble to find out why the system is as it is before you change it (don't fix it if it isn't broken). Third, your boss will have a few files of a personal or confidential nature that he will occasionally file into and personally retrieve from. These may be work related or your boss may keep one or two "home" files in his office. You should encourage your boss to do his own personal filing, making retrieval more efficient and leaving you to do the 99 percent of routine filing (yourself or delegated to your team) according to your own preferences.

With regard to the completion of forms, returns, summary sheets for submission to other departments, and so on, you should agree with your boss on those that he must complete and those that you can complete on his behalf. Further, you should agree on which of those you have completed need to be checked or approved, and which can be submitted by you directly. Where possible, you should seek to complete as many of these routine tasks as possible, removing the load from your boss's shoulders. If your boss is doing a lot of routine form filling and so on, which you are capable of doing, then he is not delegating well and you should, by example, help him to learn how to do it better.

New technology

Many bosses, particularly older bosses, are not easily impressed by advances in technology. A typical office, even a small department, may now contain a photocopier, fax machine, voice mail, the telephone system of course, a word processor, computer links to other parts of the business such as production line or accounts, and so on. There may be pagers and mobile phones available. The most modern equipment can include fax machines and voice mails installed in a car. If your boss is still insisting on using quill pen and, worse, if he is insisting you use one as well, then it is your responsibility to help drag him into at least the nineteenth century and perhaps onward into the twentieth and twenty-first centuries. The great drive in technology has been toward making it mass marketable to the workforce at large; in short, most technology is now simple to use, including even the most complex word processing programs.

By encouraging your boss to use dictation machines instead of handwritten copy or note taking and dictation, and to operate a word processor, you will, as already stated, speed up your work between yourselves. In addition, bosses should be encouraged to use equipment themselves rather than being overly dependent on you. Teach them how to use the photocopier and the fax machine. We have seen examples where a boss whose secretary was at lunch has been in a virtual panic trying to find someone who could send a fax urgently: a quarter of an hour spent looking for someone to send a two-minute fax; an inordinate waste of time. Teach your boss even to use that one nontechnological piece of equipment in the office, the wastepaper basket. We have been in an office where a boss put a large pile of papers on his secretary's desk and said, "Throw these in the basket, would you please." Operating a photocopier may take some time to learn, but we find it difficult to believe that you can rise to become a captain of industry without learning how to throw something in the wastepaper basket. On a time management basis, consider the time taken to gather up the papers, walk from one desk to another, and give an instruction that you then have to implement.

Many bosses will not use equipment of any kind for what can only be described as "snob" reasons, and these are becoming quickly outdated. Those bosses, usually much older bosses, with certain beliefs about upbringing and breeding, believe that it is somehow demeaning or servant-like to be able to operate equipment and will pretend that they have no knowledge or ability to do so, making them dependent on you. Try as gently as you can to encourage your boss into using technology by showing the advantages to him of doing so. As a practical tip, avoid mentioning anywhere along the line that his operating the technology will also save you time, though bear in mind that that is true.

One further point on encouraging the boss to use technology. Do not believe it when he keeps getting it wrong. This is the equivalent of husbands who learn to break the dirty dishes so that they won't be asked to wash them, i.e., you can keep doing it in the future. If your boss gets it wrong help him to get it right. He may continue the "tradition of nobility" attitude when you are around, but we know from experience that there will also be many times, when you are not around, when the boss will surreptitiously go over to the photocopier or the fax and operate it with the competence of a NASA-trained astronaut.

Meetings

The boss–secretary partnership in meetings is a recognition of two quite different roles. Your boss's job in a meeting is to keep the meeting alive and energized, to keep discussions focused, and to arrive at effective decisions as painlessly as possible. This involves a great deal of personal interaction in the meeting, and it is this and this alone that your boss should be concentrating on. Your task is to take away from your boss anything that lingers on his mind. You should deal with the administration and setup of the meeting, with the agenda, the taking of the minutes, and the publishing of the minutes. Your boss should not interfere in these, which should rightly be regarded as your job. We suggest that you read through Meetings, Agendas, and Minutes in Volume 1 of *The Professional Secretary* and present your proposals to your boss for approval.

Try to interface

You and your boss "meet" your clients in three ways: letters, telephones, and personally.

In responding to letters, encourage your boss to allow you to draft replies based either on dictated notes rather than fully dictated letters or on handwritten notes he makes on the incoming letter, leaving you to draft the full reply. Only very personal or highly specialized letters should be fully drafted by the boss.

With regard to telephone calls, agree with your boss on a policy of filtering that enables you to deal with the majority of calls, passing through to him only those calls that must be dealt with by the boss personally. In the section on telephone techniques (see volume 1 of *The Professional Secretary*) there are guidelines for dealing with callers seeking to speak to your boss whom your boss does not want to speak to, and guidelines for responding to inquiries without committing your boss improperly. In general, all calls to your boss should go through you and very few should need to be put through to the boss directly. If your boss is of a mind, he could have a private line directly into his own office but if so, that number should never be given out except by the boss personally.

For meeting clients, agree with your boss that you can deal with the administration of this on his behalf. You should be free to receive them as guests into your offices, where you will treat them, like guests, to appropriate comforts (refreshments, taking their coat, and telling them where the rest rooms are without them having to ask). If your boss is asking someone to meet him, then agree that it is your responsibility to make travel arrangements where appropriate, send information about getting to your offices, arrange pickups at airports, and so on. Your boss should be free of all these administrative tasks and should know that when his guest walks through the office door for the meeting the guest has been dealt with efficiently, courteously, and warmly.

Time management

Agree with your boss that you will keep her diary as well as your own. Make it a principle that you will audit your boss in order to make sure that both of you are maximizing your time management skills (see Diagnosing Time, page 103). Agree with your boss that you will make appointments to suit a general agreed preference (e.g., does your boss prefer appointments in one block, with blocks of free time, all scattered throughout the week, in the mornings, in the afternoons?).

Agree with your boss on your responsibility to remind her of the day ahead, the week ahead, and so on. Have in your diary a list of items to be brought to the boss's attention that you do on a regular basis. Protect your boss from information overload: agree with your boss that you can remove her from unwanted distribution and mailing lists (perhaps go through the initial list together).

Remember that personal power now beats job authority in terms of promotion prospects. You should therefore encourage your boss to get into personal skills training where necessary as "people-oriented" individuals are more likely to be promoted in modern companies than "task-oriented" people. (This is a very sweeping generalization but modern companies are presently moving toward operating in teams or in one-person-departments where the ability to get on with people is extremely important).

Brief your boss on the office politics of which you have become aware. This is not to suggest that you should become a spy in the office, informing on colleagues.

However, you are probably aware that the secretarial channels of communication are some of the most effective in any company and you can use those channels to keep your boss up-to-date on circumstances outside your immediate department.

Plan times for work for yourself and your boss according to your biological clocks. Many individuals reach a peak of efficiency from around 10 A.M. to noon and a trough of sluggishness at around 4 P.M. Plan to do complex, involved tasks at the peak of efficiency and routine unimportant tasks in the trough of sluggishness. These biological clock phases are fairly difficult to override and you and your boss will do best to make plans around them rather than trying to ignore them. Incidentally, daily action plans are worth saving. They can be useful reference tools—especially when you come up for review.

Make a daily action plan for both of you for tomorrow, each day before you go home. This should include appointments, priority tasks to be completed, and so on. This will give you both, in partnership, a feeling of control over your workday, which will boost your energy and performance. It will also give you a clear awareness of the tasks you will be confronting tomorrow and this will give the subconscious mind time to work overnight on problems that will arise. This is a highly effective form of time management: we often forget that our subconscious will work on problems while our conscious mind is occupied elsewhere. (How often have you woken up in the morning suddenly much clearer about a situation than you were when you went to bed the night before?) A plan for the day ahead will also help you both to avoid being sidetracked by less important tasks. You will find that a jointly agreed on action plan will make your joint communications with colleagues much more efficient and clear.

Agree on a mail review system and stick to it. Have your boss's mail put on your desk; you should go through this, passing through to your boss only those items that she must have. You deal with the rest as your own responsibility. Obviously you must decide on your boss's broader preferences before you can determine how to divide paperwork between the two of you.

Administrative assistants

There are many areas where you will work with your boss, or deputize for her, and you should agree on the most effective ways to approach these situations.

Your boss will be involved in organizing functions and meetings. You should take it on yourself to deal with the travel arrangements of delegates, their reception, refreshments, and lunches during the meeting (remembering to take account of dietary preferences). You should make sure that delegates arriving at conferences or meetings are supplied with all the paperwork they need to make their attendance most effective, and so on. In addition, if your boss is involved in the organization of less formal gatherings, parties, and so on, then you should take responsibility for their organization too. Bear in mind that if you are the head of a secretarial team, many of the functions for which you are accepting accountability can be delegated to others.

You should be able to assist your boss with personal timekeeping. Make hotel and travel bookings whenever you know that she has meetings in other cities or countries, and so on. Remind your boss of personal diary dates: spouse's birthday, anniversary, and so on. Encourage your boss to keep her personal appointments in your joint diaries so that you can remind her of those too: taking the car to the mechanic, seeing the dentist or the doctor, and so on.

Decide with your boss that you can assist in solving problems or creating ideas by acting as a sounding board for her to talk to, by collecting information that may be of use and passing it through to her, and by doing some research around the company that may be of assistance.

If your boss is involved in longer-term projects, then you should be sharing with her the administration of those projects, making sure that she is up-to-date with the best contacts and experts in the field, and obtaining for her financial and competition information. You should assist in general administration, take responsibility for printing and publication of project reports, and so on.

There will be times when you can deputize for your boss: attending meetings on her behalf and reporting back according to an agreed preference between you. You may be able to attend courses or conferences in her place, and produce a precis of the salient points.

In summary

All of the above should serve to relieve your boss of areas where he is potentially wasting time by doing work not appropriate to his level of authority. It should be highly enriching and motivating for you to have wider responsibilities where you can use your widest range of skills and your widest range of talents can be seen.

The savings in time created by an effective boss–secretary partnership are often difficult to quantify, but in the ten years or so that we have been consulting in companies of various sizes we know from the feedback from both bosses and secretaries that the effective partnership saves *a great deal* of time and effort.

Paperwork

Although much of the handling of paperwork has been covered in the guidelines on the boss–secretary partnership, it is worth summarizing a few specific points to be taken account of.

Never handle a piece of paper more than once

Avoid the habit of putting pieces of paper into in-trays, constantly picking them up and looking at them, being turned off by dealing with them, finding something else to do, and then having to pick the piece of paper up again later. Whenever you are dealing with a piece of paper, make sure that you do all you can do with it then and there and move on to the next thing.

Do–ditch–delegate

The ultimate way of dealing with every piece of paper only once is to start from its arrival on your desk, whether in the mail or otherwise, and do one of three things with it:

Do

Deal with it immediately, drafting a reply, placing it for filing, putting it into your reading tray (see Trays, following) or, if it is to be carried forward for future work, putting it into the appropriate priority tray and, when its time comes around, dealing with it once and once only.

Ditch

If you are going to throw the piece of paper into the wastepaper basket, do it now rather than later. In-trays often get full of pieces of paper that you know full well you were going to throw away eventually. Have the courage to do it at the first opportunity and prevent it from "cluttering up" your thinking and building up your in-tray frighteningly and unnecessarily.

Delegate

If the piece of paper will have to be delegated to someone else for his action, decisions, suggestions, and so on, then delegate it immediately by putting the initial of the person it is to go to on it and dropping it right into a distribution tray.

Reply on memos in

Cut down paperwork by jotting replies on memos you have received and passing them back to the originator where necessary. Do not generate another memo to reply to a first memo. Memos by their very nature are usually immediate, and once dealt with are never referred to again. Try to get out of the habit of filing memos and other documents that you know you will not need to refer to in the future (how often have you stood at your desk with a piece of paper in one hand and a hole puncher in the other before filing that piece of paper, knowing, certainly, that no one will ever look at it again?). In certain types of companies—attorneys' offices, insurance companies, and so on—there is a greater requirement for maintaining historic documentation, but make sure that your decision to retain any piece of paper is based on need rather than caution.

Get yourself and your boss off mailing and distribution lists

Even before you "do–ditch–delegate," you are better off not receiving paper you don't want in the first place.

Use the telephone

Generating paperwork takes more time than using the telephone. For immediate queries or responses, and where no documentation is required, get into the habit of making telephone calls instead of creating memos and letters. Where this is done within a company, it requires a policy of openness and trust, which you should help to foster within the company by leading by example. There may be less opportunity to do this between companies, where a higher level of documentation may be necessary.

Have small in-trays and a big wastepaper basket

We encountered two very radical paperwork tips, which we would not necessarily recommend because they are somewhat reckless and in some companies would be rather dangerous, but which we include here partly for humor and partly because we are assured by those who live by these rules that, reckless or not, they work.

The first of these was the statement by one manager that she opens all her mail two weeks late. In her experience, over half the letters she opens have, by that time, answered themselves already or become irrelevant, without ever having affected her or her department.

The second rather sweeping time management technique to deal with paperwork was suggested by a manager who came back from vacation to find his desk full of paperwork and who positioned the wastepaper basket at the end of the desk, tipped the desk up, and slid everything into it. "If there is anything important in there, they will write again", he told us.

Perhaps we should point out that such radical decisions are really management's prerogative, rather than yours, but you could always experiment with these theories with your mail at home!

Trays

You will need more than an in-tray and an out-tray if you are going to be an efficient time manager. You will need several trays, preferably not cluttering up your desk but on shelves behind you. These are trays into which at various times in the day you will put various papers to be dealt with in specific time-planned ways. These papers may arrive there directly from the mail (do–ditch–delegate), from others, or from your boss, or they may be on their way out to others or for you at a later time. The trays are as follows.

File

Any papers to be filed, whether they have just arrived in the mail or have been generated by yourself or others, should be placed in this tray. You should delegate to a member of your team, where appropriate, that he has the duty to take that filing tray and file its contents without having to ask your permission. He should organize the clearing of your filing tray in his own prioritization and grid of urgency. His objective is to keep this tray empty on, say, a weekly basis.

Mail

Any letters or documents that are to be mailed, or sent down to the mail room, should be put into this tray and, again, a member of your staff delegated to deal with it without needing to ask your permission. Her objective is to keep that tray empty on a daily basis and certainly to clear it at the end of each day, having discussed the requirements of the mail room for each day's delivery to the post office.

Pass on

Any documents that are to be read by others should be initialed by yourself and then put into the "pass on" tray for delivery to the next person on the distribution list. Memos or documents that you originate and that are to go to others should also be placed in this tray. Each document should have a clear indication, perhaps a "post-it" note, of whom it should be passed on to. A member of your staff should be delegated to keep the tray clear on an agreed routine basis.

Awaiting information

There will always be areas of work where you cannot make progress because you have requested information from others that is yet to arrive. Any such documents should be put into the "awaiting information" tray. Preferably keep each discrete piece of work in a separate display folder.

Important tip 1

Effective time management of this tray depends on you putting notes in your diary to follow up requests. For every display folder or document in the "awaiting information" tray, you should have a diary note stating the time when you expect the information or when you have agreed it should be received. If the information is not with you by that time, you should vigorously contact the person from whom you requested the information. Make it clear that you are not the sort of person who should be ignored or made a low priority in someone else's grid of urgency. If she has made a commitment to you to supply information, then you must make it clear that you expect those commitments to be met. If you vigorously follow up information requested, this tray will clear itself on a regular basis; if you do not then it will mount up unnecessarily, become a source of irritation, and be a cause of missed deadlines and missed opportunities.

Important tip 2

Every item in your awaiting information tray should be somewhere on your grid of urgency and your list of priorities. Make sure that changes in circumstances bring delayed work, for whatever reason, to the appropriate point in both the grid and the list.

Read

There will be a number of documents that are for you to read. They may be circulated on distribution lists through the company, they may be articles you have located in magazines or books or that have been copied for you for information, and so on. Do not read these as and when they arrive but rather put them, as soon as you get them, into the "read" tray and make note sometime during the week to clear the tray by reading and synthesizing these documents. Having planned time to do the reading, make it a time when you are comfortable and when you can read in a relaxed and preferably uninterrupted state. You will learn more and clear this tray more efficiently this way than if you try to snatch bits of reading here and there throughout the day. Your objective is to keep this tray empty on a weekly basis by planning time to deal with it regularly.

Important tip 1
The contents of this tray should always be carried around with you whenever there is the possibility of being delayed during traveling, when attending conferences, meetings, and so on. This is a perfect tray for turning red time into green time.

Important tip 2
You may decide not to read your trays during work time at all but instead, replace a newspaper you did not want to read anyway with the contents of your tray during your commuting. This is also a good green time use of regular traveling.

Telephone

We have suggested that you plan to make certain telephone calls when you are in the right frame of mind and the right place and when you are prepared for them. Put your notes of these telephone calls into your telephone tray and make sure that you plan time each day for clearing this tray. Remember our guidelines to clear that tray effectively: before making telephone calls, you should make sure that you have all the relevant papers on your desk where you can access them quickly. Your telephone call will then be efficient, effective, and timesaving.

Priority trays

You should have separate trays for your grid of urgency tasks, i.e., trays for the important and urgent, the unimportant but urgent, the important but nonurgent, and the unimportant and nonurgent. Make sure that your diaries contain target times for completion of all of these trays and make sure that you have communicated effectively to your own staff those tasks that they should be dealing with on your behalf. Where you have delegated work, encourage your staff to have similar sets of trays into which such paperwork is placed.

You may have other specific suggestions for trays depending on the type of work you are doing and the type of company you are doing it in. The golden rule is that the more trays you have, with sensible purposes, the more efficient your paperwork and therefore your time management.

Diary

In addition to keeping your boss's diary of personal and business appointments, reminders, and so on, you should keep an efficient diary of your own containing more than simply appointments or notes for your boss. Your own diary should contain information related to the clearance of your various trays. For every item in your "awaiting information" tray, you should have a diary note on the day when you expect to receive that information. If not received, you should follow it up vigorously and become known as someone who cannot be ignored.

For each day in your diary, you should have time planned to deal with your read tray and your telephone tray. You should also have specific entries in your diary for each item in your various grid of urgency or priority trays, so that you are working to self-imposed deadlines for all major aspects of your work. Remember, of course, that your job is still one largely at the whim of your boss and therefore the amount of time that you can specifically designate for yourself for clearing your trays is limited (see The Workplace, following).

Your diary should also contain notes of any time you have been promised feedback for a delegated task or project or any time when you have made an agreement to meet someone to discuss his progress. For example, in the guidelines for giving constructive criticism, we suggest that when giving constructive criticism, you also agree on a target time to review progress; this should be entered in your diary and strictly adhered to.

Note that your diary need not be literally a bound diary but can be a loose-leaf file with sections for daily, weekly, monthly, and annually, each having very detailed lists.

The Workplace

Good time management of your workplace can be summed up in two words: tidiness and planning.

For tidiness, we suggest that your desk should be totally clear at all times other than for the piece of work you are doing at the present moment. All your upcoming work should be in your trays kept on shelves away from your desk. We would suggest that even your telephone and desk ornaments be placed on a side desk so that you have a full clear operating surface. The phrase "a messy desk causes stress" is a good working guideline. Although we have seen very good managers with very messy desks, there has never been any case where we felt that good managerial ability came about because of the messy desk; rather it was despite it. A messy desk only creates a situation where a considerable amount of the day (it could add up to an hour or more) is spent lifting pieces of paper looking for other pieces of paper, and so on. There is nothing you can do in a messy disorganized office that you cannot do more efficiently in a tidy organized office.

With regard to planning, you cannot be expected to keep your trays clear and deal with your grid of urgency or your list of prioritized tasks if you do not plan time to deal with them. Although as a secretary you must accept that you are to some extent reactive to the needs of your boss, an effective boss–secretary partnership must recognize that you need a certain amount of time for yourself. This time for yourself should be "closed door" and your own subordinates—and your boss—should respect the closed door as being your way of dealing with problems, allowing you to have an "open door" during most of the week. We suggest that you arrange with your boss to have a minimum of one hour and preferably two hours per day without interruption. Although this quite often astonishes secretaries and even frightens bosses, where we have done training in boss–secretary partnerships (with both parties in the training room), the feedback has always indicated that both parties found it productive once they got used to it.

In order to have a completely clear hour or two, you have to make sure that everyone knows you should not be interrupted; you may use humor to do this. One secretary hung a sign on her closed door that simply said "Here reside dragons . . ." She was certainly no dragon and she was recognized as a very good team leader, but the humor of the message was very clear to those around her and her closed door was respected. In an open plan office, it is more difficult to close the door and the most effective suggestion we heard of was the secretary who had a picture of a rottweiler growling fiercely, which she would put on her desk at times when she was not to be disturbed. Again, this was respected and her time management was very effective.

During the one or two hours of closed door time, you plan the appropriate time to deal with your trays, make your telephone calls, and so on. The one interruption you cannot always control is the telephone. But even here we would suggest, as we have done in several companies, where it has been very successful, that you make a back-up arrangement with another secretary, where for one hour you will take her calls and for another hour she will take yours. With the exception of the occasional extremely urgent call, most callers will understand a delay of one hour or more in your returning their call (and remember to make your outgoing calls in the way described above).

When scheduling the use of your one or two planned hours, remember to include in there appropriate breaks for yourself when you can relax, review the day past, and consider the day ahead. Five minutes' thinking can save an hour's unproductive effort.

"Play the game"

Secretaries are conditioned to believe that every minute of their day is at the whim of someone else (usually their boss). You must change that attitude in yourself and your boss, preferably by example. Ask your boss to "play the game" for a month and demonstrate to her the significant effect on the efficiency of your office and your partnership of doing so. We have yet to find a boss who has asked her secretary to go back to the old way of doing things once this has proved to be successful.

Diagnosing Time

In order to manage time, you must first know what you are presently doing with it. Record what you are doing in appropriate blocks of time: half an hour, one hour, half a day, and so on. Keep an accurate record of how you spend your days for, say, three weeks. You should then diagnose your results, seeking to eliminate any task you are doing that adds nothing to the overall effectiveness of you or your office. Of the tasks that are being done, ask the following questions: What is being done, where is it being done, when is it being done, who does it, and how is it being done? Then ask "why?" of all these questions. From this, you can determine tasks that you should be delegating or tasks that you are delegating improperly. Repeat this diagnosis on a regular basis, at least twice a year, to make sure that your time management skills are maintained.

In diagnosing time, you should identify all the activities that could be done by someone else as well as you can do them, if not better. You should identify those activities that are essential, those activities that are routine, those activities that must be carried out by yourself, and those activities that could be carried out by others or by you and another together. For every task, make sure that you know where it should have fallen into your grid of urgency and priority list and make sure that you did deal with it in the appropriate area. If you dealt with a task inappropriately (e.g., you dealt urgently and importantly with a task that was not important or not urgent), then be sure to learn from that mistake and be more disciplined in dealing with such tasks in the future.

Exercise 3: Self-audit

The self-audit is designed to determine if you are an effective time manager, or whether you represent a barrier to effective time management. There are two aspects to the audit (outlined below) and for maximum efficiency you should complete this for yourself and also ask a trusted and valued friend or colleague to complete the same form for you. Compare the two results and pay particular attention to areas where you and your friend or colleague have a quite different view of the way you act.

Yes   No

1. Are you busy sorting our insignificant problems that are preventing you from dealing with more important priorities?
2. Do you find that you easily make excuses to delay work you don't want to do?
3. Does hard work make you feel virtuous?

Yes No

4. Do you feel guilty when you are not active?
5. Do you put off urgent and important tasks until the last moment?
6. Do you fail to take vacations and long weekends?
7. Do you take work home regularly?
8. Are your various trays piling up without control, e.g., your reading tray or telephone tray?
9. Have you been late for appointments, missed appointments, or failed to notify your boss of an appointment that he has then missed or been late for?
10. Do you fail to take proper breaks from work?
11. Are you free to be interrupted during the day?
12. Does work bring you pleasure and satisfaction?
13. Do you set six-month, five-year, and lifetime goals?
14. Do you set short- and long-term objectives?
15. Do you think you should be working harder?
16. Do you feel that you are under stress, without being able to define the causes?
17. Are you having fun?
18. Do you live to work (as opposed to work to live)?
19. Do you regularly fail to meet your objectives and goals?
20. Do you feel full of energy?
21. Do you thrive on competition and challenge?
22. Do you try to do more than one thing at a time?
23. Is there conflict in your personal and professional life? (Ask your spouse or partner to answer this one as well as yourself.)

Between yourself and the other person completing this questionnaire, you should find some surprises, a few of which might shock you. Consider those surprises carefully and bear in mind that other people's views of you are likely to be more objective if you can trust them to be honest with you. There is of course no right or wrong answer to these questions; nor is there a score that tells you whether you are a good or bad time manager. The material in this part of the book will tell you that, and guide you to better skills. However, the answers to this self-audit will give you some idea of your personal starting point in, first, your attitude toward time and, second, your specific issues at work.

Be Systematic and Logical

There is one further guideline to consider, based on the fact that you have just one pair of eyes and one pair of hands. Do not try to do many things at once; having made your list of priorities for the day deal with them systematically and logically. It was said of Charles Schwab, who created one of the largest independent steel-producing companies in the world, that the greatest lesson he ever learned was taught to him by a time management consultant who told him, "Each evening write down the things you have to do tomorrow and number them in order of importance. First thing in the morning start working on item 1 and continue with it until you have finished it. Then start on item 2. Then the same with item 3, and so on. Do not be worried if you haven't finished them all. If you can't do it by this method you can't do it by any other." Schwab apparently sent the consultant a check for $25,000, and claimed that this was the most profitable lesson he ever learned in his career.

Remember that with proper preplanning and proper organization in accordance with the guidelines we have given, you will clear your list most days and you will catch up on occasional crises very quickly, keeping on top of the work. You will spend the rest of your working life feeling in control and energized, and, we hope, enjoying your time in the office.

PART 3

The Lone Arranger

Some secretaries, far from having a team, are in fact expected virtually to run small companies without assistance. The boss is an expert in some field, perhaps a printer, accountant, or builder, and is often absent from the office. The secretary—the Lone Arranger—becomes virtually the entire office team. The Lone Arranger is, in fact, all but the owner of the business and needs to know more or less what an owner needs to know. The areas covered in this part of the book refer to the most common questions and situations such secretaries have identified to us in our courses.

Managing Your Relationship with Your Boss

You will often be working on your own, but you will also, on occasion, be working very closely with your boss. It is therefore very important that you learn to manage your relationship with your boss. Apart from your family, partner, and close friends, your boss is probably the biggest influence on your life. He has the power to make you happy by boosting your moral, energizing you by giving you responsibility and new challenges, and positively motivating you. And, of course, he is responsible for your salary. Conversely, your boss can upset you by unfair criticism, setting impossible work deadlines, ignoring your suggestions, and generally refusing to accept the contributions that you make to the firm.

Consider your boss as your most important customer. His output will very often be dependent on your input. You must see yourself as in partnership with your boss, with mutual understanding and recognition. Being a good secretary does not mean acting in a subordinate way, it means a relationship of mutual respect based on a set of agreed working rights and clear demarcation of who is responsible for what. You have a duty of care to give your boss not only your work duties, but also the best possible professional advice.

Acceptable and unacceptable behavior

In larger organizations there is what is called a "corporate culture." A simple definition of culture is "the way we do things around here." That corporate culture is a set of values, attitudes, and rules that define what is acceptable and what is not. The Lone Arranger with one boss will have no such culture at the outset; a small business equivalent will have to be developed over time. Of course, if either the boss or the secretary has come from other and larger organizations, then they will bring to the firm facets of that other culture.

The way we behave is based on what rights we think we have. A working professional relationship between two people means deciding on the boundary rules and the rights that the individuals can exercise. In a very small firm, there will be one set of rights that may not necessarily be applicable to a larger organization. Some of the rights for a small firm could be as follows:

- the right to communicate openly views and ideas concerning the running of the firm;
- the right to be consulted on issues that affect you;
- the right to say yes or no at appropriate times;
- the right not to know or understand something;
- the right to change your mind;
- the right to make mistakes, and to have the opportunity to correct them;
- the right to challenge ideas.

These suggested rights, and others, should be discussed with your boss, and can be experimented with by testing the boundary rules.

A more difficult set of boundary rules is the personal transactions between you and your boss. It is still the case that many male bosses marry their female secretaries, and many bosses leave their partners for their secretaries. If you are spending eight hours or more each day with one person, then a bond arises that can lead to friendship, and sometimes to attraction. Depending on the personal circumstances of you both, this can be positive and healthy, and lead to a "fairy-tale ending." But if your personal circumstances should not encourage that interaction, or you simply wish to make clear that such a relationship is not on your agenda, then you will both have to define a mutually agreed on culture that you can happily live in.

Attitudes and values

Attitudes are the ways we think of ideas and issues. Values are personal standards of behavior. Attitudes and values govern the way we live our lives and although they can be changed, it is a difficult process and takes time. People with totally different attitudes and values will often find it difficult to live together. If they continue in a relationship, it will only survive if both parties learn to ignore and/or not to respond to attitudinal and value differences.

When you are being interviewed for a job as Lone Arranger, use part of the interview to make sure that you and your prospective boss can work together. In a one-on-one relationship, we often assume wrongly that we are basically similar people; the interview process is a two-way communication exercise and you are entitled to ask questions of your prospective boss to see if you can work with her in such a close, symbiotic, relationship. Asking your potential boss for her views on a range of work and social issues will enable you to form an opinion, and your responses to his or her questions will enable her to form an opinion as to whether you are compatible and able to work closely together.

The office setup

Where possible, it is better that you and your boss have separate offices, or at the least partitioning so that visual contact is kept to the minimum. Day-to-day constant visual contact, with all the body language that goes with it, is the first stage of forming close human relationships. Body language, such as the nod, wink, frown, smile, and so on, creates a common language almost like a child's secret codes with friends; you and your boss become like one another. Your attention to many issues will also create a strong and close bond and your knowledge of each other can make it difficult to maintain a professional working relationship. The more you have your own space, the less dependent on each other you become.

What do you call each other?

Fortunately we have moved a long way since the formality and class-ridden culture of Edwardian and post-Edwardian society. There are now guidelines that companies have developed as acceptable. The following would seem to be the norm in many organizations. In front of customers and people who have dealings with your firm (e.g., bankers or creditors), you should call your boss Mr. Mrs. Miss, or Ms. (for women, the choice of the three alternatives should be their decision). Your boss should do the same, but with your agreement, your given name can be used. Age may influence the best style. In most workplaces, given names will probably be used. It is advisable to avoid nicknames or pet names that may suggest an intimacy you do not have, should not have, and should not project. It would be more than just irritating for the wife of a male boss to hear a female secretary announce over the phone, when putting her call through, "It's your wife, honey."

The boss and you

Assuming that you are only seeking to develop and maintain a professional working relationship, your private lives should be kept separate and at a distance. It is necessary for you to draw a clear line around your normal work role, what you will do to help out if the workload gets behind, and what is not acceptable to you under any circumstances. The following questions will help you to find out how close the relationship has become already. For new secretaries, some of these areas may well ring warning bells if they should arise.

Does your boss

	Yes	No
1. Ask you to pick up his children from school?		
2. Ask you to obtain birthday cards and/or presents for his family?		
3. Invite you to his home for a family meal?		
4. Invite you to join him on business trips?		
5. Invite you for after-work drinks in the office?		
6. Discuss his private and personal problems with you?		
7. Invite you out to lunch on a regular basis?		
8. Drive you to and from work?		
9. Buy you gifts, flowers, cologne?		
10. Compliment you on the way you dress and look?		
11. Ever make overt innuendo and provocative remarks of a sexual nature?		
12. Find any excuse to get near to you, brush past you, and accidentally touch you?		

9–12 yes answers: As you know, you are too close to your boss to have a long-term working relationship.

6–8 answers: You have allowed a close personal relationship to develop and you may now find it hard to pull back.

3–5 answers: You are enjoying a healthy and professional working relationship with your boss.

Confidentiality and boundary rules

Working closely with one person and running the office on your own, and therefore being the center of communications for your boss, will mean that you will learn a great deal about private matters relating to your boss. The way you handle the knowledge you gain will be a matter for you and your conscience, though we suggest some important guidelines below.

If, for instance, your boss is having a secret affair, what do you do? How do you treat that special friend if she is a regular caller by telephone or in person? What do you do if your boss asks you to lie to his spouse (e.g., saying he is on a business trip when that is not true)? These are potentially very awkward and embarrassing situations.

The best advice we can offer is to make sure that you sort out the boundary rules with your boss at the beginning, or at the first opportunity. You must be ready to discuss at least some of the following issues.

- Accept that your boss must make his own rules for a private life, and agree between yourselves that you will respect how he wishes to conduct that private life within the grounds of common decency.
- Agree that you will treat all friends—special or otherwise—in a professional and business-like manner.
- Make clear that you will not deliberately lie to anyone about his movements or travel arrangements. You are entitled to self-respect.
- Agree that you will, if necessary, adopt a position of "I do not know" when challenged.
- Get agreement that your boss must respect your right not to know certain private matters, and that you will not be put on the spot over such matters.

And remember, do not involve your boss in your private life.

Your boss, the law, and self-regulatory bodies

Another area to consider in your relationship with your boss is the law in general and the ever-increasing number of self-regulatory bodies. If, for instance, your boss is an attorney, then the American Bar Association is the regulatory body for that profession. It draws up a set of rules and regulations that your boss must abide by in order to retain the right to practice. A professional secretary is not expected to know the letter of the law, but certainly over a period of time, you would become aware of the rules governing a particular profession. In the unlikely event that your boss does break the law, or transgress the professional regulations, how should you act?

Because the Lone Arranger is the communications channel for this business, she is more likely than most secretaries to hear of any disciplinary threats and to be aware of the circumstances that might have led to the investigation. In the case of breaches of the law, the position is clear. If your boss has control over clients' monies, and steals from those clients, then you must report that to the police. By all means, give your boss a chance to return the money immediately, but remember as a professional person yourself you have a duty of care toward your customers and clients in the same way as your boss. Similarly, cheating the Internal Revenue Service, should not be acceptable to you.

You must be sure you conduct yourself in an appropriate and professional way. In the event that your boss commits breaches or offenses, you could be called to court, or hearings, as part of a prosecution case. If that has to happen, make sure that you are a witness and not a co-defendant!

A breach of self-regulatory conduct, however, is very often difficult to understand and discover. Should you do so, then we suggest the following course of action:

1. On discovery of a serious breach of professional conduct or professional regulations, immediately see your boss and inform him of what you have found out.
2. Ask for an explanation of what has arisen and what he or she now proposes to do.
3. Make a file note of all conversations.
4. Do not get implicated in any way. Certainly do not assist in any cover-ups.

5. If your boss refuses to take corrective action, then inform your boss that you now need to get professional advice.
6. Without naming any individuals, take advice from the compliance section of the appropriate self-regulatory body.
7. If the matter is very serious, get advice from your lawyer.
8. If necessary, resign.

Loyalty to your boss

We have said previously that you should not get involved in your boss's private life. But if you have a correct professional relationship, it is also normal for friendship and respect to develop. What do you do then if your boss starts to develop potentially destructive habits, such as very heavy drinking, drug abuse, or gambling?

You must point out to your boss that you have noticed what is happening and suggest that he gets professional help. If, however, your boss refuses—and most will to begin with—then you will have to decide whether you can professionally continue working with your boss, who is heading toward destruction. Remember that your professional reputation may be at risk, and your job certainly is because if he loses the company, there will be no job.

You must also consider the aspect of your own physical security. If you are female and alone in the office with your boss, who is a potentially violent, excessive drinking, man, then you may be at risk inside your job. If you identify with this, start reading the classified sections immediately.

Day-to-day relationship

Because you are working in a one-to-one relationship with your boss, you are in the front line for mood swings, criticism, frustration, and disappointments, as well as excitement and celebrations. Remember to mirror your boss's good moods as best you can. If you have just landed a large contract, then be excited with him. You need never mirror bad moods: by all means share frustration and disappointment, but do not get mutually depressed. All people get moody and you cannot live together for eight hours a day without living with each other's moods. Learn to respect your boss's feelings and learn the tricks that can snap your boss out of his bad moods. Your boss should care enough to learn the same about you.

If your boss criticizes you, do not get angry. Avoid confrontation and a stand-up argument; concentrate on the part of the criticism that relates to your work. Think about any work criticisms and offer your side of the story, in detail. Tell your boss what changes you intend to make to yourself (e.g., training) or to the work methods or systems to make sure that it will not happen again. If your boss is upset with you, don't hide or avoid the issue. Confront your boss and ask him to be open with you about the reason for the upset.

Surprise your boss

All relationships can grow old and stale unless you work to put a little zest into them. This is true of professional relationships as well as personal ones.

Don't get into the habit of habit. Change routines, change the office layout. Suggest new ideas for working methods, new programs for the computer, or a new image, logo, and design. Keep abreast of new product or service developments in the press and trade magazines. Cut them out for your boss and ask for comments. Solicit customers and clients, get their views and pass them on to your boss. If time permits, go to trade or product shows. Network with other secretaries to get new ideas for the office. Set yourself some achievable key performance indicators so that you can report them to your boss on a regular basis. Communicate good news and always be ready to congratulate your boss (there may be no one else to do so).

Relationships have to be worked at, and the secret of a good relationship is honest and open communication. Working in a small firm can be fun as well as rewarding. For the Lone Arranger, being in control, making decisions, developing the business, and keeping close customer/client contact are the highest form of motivation.

Running the Office

As well as the professional secretarial and organizational skills that you have acquired, you will have to learn many more new general and specialist tasks if you are to run the business on your own on a day-to-day basis without the need to bring in outside help. Some of these tasks and skills will be shared with your boss, but from our experience, the boss will want to concentrate her energy on areas that produce income for the business and to hand over as soon as possible all the day-to-day operational matters to you. Your willingness to take on these tasks will depend on your training and previous job experiences. Whatever the state of play, it is useful to agree with your boss on a schedule determining what jobs you intend to take on and when. In the meantime, arrange for training if necessary.

Financial skills

Cash flow is the lifeblood of all businesses. In the long run, firms can make all the profits they want and still go out of business through lack of cash (mostly from unpaid sales) to pay the bills, pay the wages, and repay any loans. It is essential that you and your boss acquire necessary financial skills as quickly as possible. In very brief outline, the basic financial tasks are as follows.

- Invoice daily, weekly, or monthly all those customers to whom you have sold goods and services since the last invoice you sent them. An invoice is a bill on company letterhead that describes financial information. All invoices have to be numbered in sequence. Terms and conditions of trading should be printed on the back of the invoice.

- Weekly or monthly, draw up a statement of account between your firm and your customer, clearly setting out by invoice number and date what is owed to you. Highlight sums overdue.
- Debt collection is a very important job, and your task is to collect all monies owed to the firm within the agreed payment terms. You will need to agree with your boss on a policy for debt collection. This policy will address such issues as who is responsible for contacting which particular customer, what pressure can be put on the customer, when you stop supplying goods or services if the customer continues not to pay, and when you hand over the debt to a debt collection agency or a lawyer.
- Deposit all cash and checks daily.
- Pay all bills as and when they fall due. For ease of computing and administration, a lot of small companies pay all their bills on one particular day of the month. This may be a useful routine, especially if your boss has to sign all the checks, which can be done at one meeting.
- Pay the wages/salary to you and your boss and amounts due to any subcontractors, as agreed on with your boss.

One of the most important skills is managing the cash flow of the business. This means keeping an up-to-date running record of monies coming into, and out of, your business bank account. It is important not only that you collect money and pay your bills on time, but also that you do not become overdrawn or go above your line of credit agreed with your bank. Keeping the cash flow up-to-date and in your control is best done by keeping the cash journals. At the least, keep a daily detailed statement of movements into and out of the bank account, so that you know every day what the fund's position is.

A convenient way of paying some bills is by standing order, or direct debit. This has the advantage of spreading the payment more evenly through the year, and reducing the number of checks that have to be drawn. Keep a diary, card index, or computer list of all direct debit and standing orders; do not forget to take them into account when calculating your cash position.

If you calculate that your firm will soon run out of cash, and bills are looming, then discuss the matter with your boss at once. She may wish to contact the bank to arrange a temporary increase in the line of credit or may authorize you to contact customers to collect money and, if necessary, offer a settlement discount for quick payment.

Financial control of a small firm is not difficult, and is certainly interesting. The main trick is to keep all your books and records up-to-date and your boss fully informed of what is happening. Depending on the number of transactions involved, we suggest a weekly or monthly financial review meeting with your boss. Remember that you are the finance director of this small business.

Some Lone Arrangers will also be required to keep the account ledgers—either can be kept manually or on computer. Given time and self-motivation it is well worth investing in a basic bookkeeping course. These are run by local colleges, but can also be conducted by correspondence schools and private study. Bookkeeping is a valuable and transferable skill and is probably a must for the modern Lone Arranger.

As the business grows and the turnover of the firm increases, you may get involved in more detailed accounting functions, such as keeping records in order to complete the quarterly reports for lenders or investors. At this point, you may find it necessary to hire a part-time bookkeeper.

Dealing with the bank

Bank managers tell us that banks like to deal with people, not account numbers. So, at the outset of the business or on joining your boss, make sure you are introduced to the person at the bank who will be looking after the firm's account. Contrary to popular belief, most banks are friendly and helpful, and as long as you keep to your agreements and banking arrangements with them, you will have no problems at all.

Always keep your bank fully informed of what is happening in the business: not only are they interested, but you will help them to understand your accounts and your future business plans. Try never to surprise your bank. If you do realize that inadvertently you are going over the established line of credit, then let them know at once, and at the same time inform them of what corrective action you are taking to rectify the position. Many banks have small business advisors who can advise you and your boss on the development of your business. Banks produce some very good and clear publications on a wide variety of subjects such as exporting and cash flow models, with easy-to-use suggested formats.

Banks also offer a wide variety of financial services, including insurance, and pensions. Do remember that banks charge for advice like any other business, and do not get into the habit of contacting them unless it is really necessary.

Dealing with insurance companies

There are many insurance companies, making the choice of one difficult. The range of products is so varied that some sort of guidance for the beginner is useful. The options open to you are: you can go directly to an insurance company for coverage, or you can go to an independent broker, your bank, and specialist insurers particularly relating to your trade. The commercial rule is: shop around and always get more than one quote.

The types of insurance you may have to consider are as follows:

- key person life insurance;
- private health insurance;
- travel insurance;
- personal accident insurance;
- office policy insurance—fire, theft, equipment, furniture;
- public liability insurance;
- car, van, or truck insurance;

- professional liability insurance;
- goods-in-transit insurance;
- special and all risks insurance.

For the small business we recommend your bank and/or a reputable independent broker who is a member of a regulatory body. Although you may pay a slightly higher premium for their services, you will save time by not having to deal with different insurance companies, and a lot of policies can be combined: an office combined policy can cover fire, theft, public liability, and all and special risks, if not more.

Always request sensible and reasonable coverage and resist spending money on nonessential coverage. Read the policy documents very carefully. If in doubt, ask your broker or advisor to explain the small print to you. When filling in a proposal form for coverage, remember the *uberrimae fidei* (utmost good faith) rule; this means that you must make full disclosure of all material facts at the time of entering into an insurance contract, or the contract may be voidable by the other party. If you run into difficulties with claims, then go back to your bank or broker, and if necessary contact the insurance ombudsman.

Dealing with lawyers

A cynic once remarked, "never involve lawyers in legal matters." When two farmers go to court over ownership of a cow, only the lawyer milks it. In short, lawyers are expensive, and the legal process does take a long time. Only the very rich should pick up the phone and contact their lawyer at the drop of a hat. Certainly any approach that avoids the legal process should be tried first. However, in some circumstances you may need to take legal advice and the following guidelines may be of help.

- If you do not already have a lawyer, your local bar association and lawyer directory can provide you with a list of lawyers in your area.
- When contacting attorneys in the first instance, always ask if they have the necessary experience to deal with the type of legal work you need. A divorce lawyer may not be the best suited for a claim against a computer company whose product does not work.
- Although it is often well worth investing in an hour of an attorney's time in order to get a consultation, always ask for a cheaper option. A good attorney will always advise you to recover small debts through the small claims court rather than use his firm.
- For essential legal work, like contract writing, shop around and get a quote.
- For essential but risky legal work, offer to pay your attorney's fees on a win-or-lose basis, i.e., your lawyer will get only a percentage of what you win.

Do remember that lawyers are necessary to safeguard you and the business. The slow legal process is not particularly their fault, and they are on your side. From talking to lawyers about what advice they would give to a small business, we have found that the consensus seems to be:

- never go to court unless it is really necessary;
- always settle with the other party if possible;
- explore all other options, e.g., ombudsmen or small claims courts, before engaging in the legal process;
- never take a "man of straw" to court (you win, but you get nothing);
- never take legal advice from a nonqualified person.

Dealing with accountants

Being in a small business it may not be necessary for you to engage the services of an accountant. Sole proprietorships and partnerships, unlike incorporated companies, are not subject to statutory audits, and can submit tax returns themselves.

The IRS will require an annual statement from you setting out income less expenditure (profit and loss statement) and in some cases a statement of assets and liabilities (balance sheet). The rules governing the type and detail of the information required can be obtained from federal and local tax offices. We recommend that if you hire an accountant, you should hire a qualified one, i.e., a member of one of the recognized professional accountant organizations.

Whether or not you wish to hire an accountant—or the extent you use one—will often depend on the accounting skills of you and your boss, i.e., to what stage you can compile the necessary books of account, so that a set of accurate accounts can be extracted. In any event, taxation is a very specialized field of professional work and from our experience a good accountant will normally save her fee by pointing out areas where you can legitimately claim tax relief, such as profit and loss items and capital allowances. New systems of tax and reporting of profits for all small businesses almost seemed designed to put all of the work onto the trader, and to create a situation where avoiding interest penalties is almost impossible. It is becoming increasingly difficult to operate a small business without an accountant's advice.

When you engage an accountant, we recommend the following.

- The best way to get an accountant is by recommendation; talk to your colleagues and friends.
- If you do not know an accountant, professional accountant organizations, such as The American Institute of Certified Public Accountants, may offer a list of practicing members in your area.
- When interviewing prospective accountants, establish whether they specialize in small company work, and make sure they have clients in similar businesses to yourselves on their lists.
- Fees are by negotiation and will often depend upon the state of your firm's books and records. Obviously the more you can prepare your accounts in the office, the lower the fee. If you wish to shop around to obtain comparative quotes, ask the

accountants for their average hourly rate for your type of work. This will give you a useful benchmark for comparison.

- Make sure you explain to your accountant who is responsible for what. You may well agree to produce your accounting records to trial balance stage, and the accountant agrees to produce the profit and loss statement and balance sheet, and to deal with all taxation matters. All accountants should issue an agreed contract that you both sign, setting out the terms and conditions of employment.

Accountants can also offer professional help of a general business and financial nature: for instance, the most efficient way to purchase an asset (lease or bank loan); how to draw up a business plan or cash flow statement; advice on investments and borrowing. Again, remember that advice has to be paid for.

Your accountant is on your side; accountants usually have invaluable contacts with local banks, and others that can be made available to you. A good accountant can also advise when it is time to call in a specialist.

Dealing with suppliers

In the course of the day-to-day administration of your firm, you will be purchasing goods and services from many different suppliers. The rule of good procurement is to investigate the market and apply the policy of money for value and value for money. Money for value means that cheap is never cheap; you should have the authority from your boss to spend what is necessary to get the right goods and services. Value for money means that you will buy the best at the most competitive price.

For local purchases, e.g., small business supplies, it is well worth identifying good local suppliers. They will appreciate your business, and loyalty, and will offer you in turn a quality service. In order to minimize your bookkeeping entries, consider opening a credit account. Remember to pay them promptly. There are some very well-organized, discounted mail order services available for, say, stationery. Investigate these because they can be very useful, not just in saving money, but because they usually deliver free as well. Depending on what business you are in, your boss may well be a member of a trade association, e.g., builders, electricians, real estate agents, or lawyers. These organizations may have negotiated discounts with retail suppliers for members, which can be advantageous for larger capital items, such as computers or motor vehicles.

Maintenance and repairs

If you lease premises, then the landlord of your office is normally responsible for the outside maintenance of the building. Your firm will be responsible for the inside. Most leases are granted on condition that you keep the inside in good order and at the end of the lease hand the property back in as good a state of repair as you found it.

Unless you are a do-it-yourself enthusiast—or your firm happens to be a builder or decorator—it will be necessary for you to find some good local tradesmen, or a good, general handyman who can do all the small and essential jobs. In the first instance, ask your neighbors to see whom they use. Always take a selection of quotes to make sure you are getting competitive prices.

If you wish to make changes to the office (knocking down walls, building walls, etc.), discuss it first with your landlord or managing agent. This will save a lot of trouble at the end of the lease. When you rent new offices, invest in a few photographs of them so that at the end of the lease you can remind the landlord of what state they were in; again this will help to iron out any differences when you vacate.

Employment agencies

From time to time, it may be necessary to use the services of an employment agency to get temporary staff for very busy times, your own illness or vacations, or special needs. In order to get a suitable person, you will need to state your exact requirements in some detail. For this reason, we suggest that you have at least an outline job description of your own job to offer when discussing a temp with an agency. Recruitment agencies charge extremely high fees, but you can shop around and negotiate discounts, especially if you agree to use only one agency for your requirements.

Remember that temporary staff will not necessarily have the same skill base as you. The Lone Arranger is virtually an entrepreneur; most secretaries at temporary agencies are trained in more limited office-based skills, typing, reception, and so on.

Rental car companies, executive taxis, and others

It will be necessary at times to use outside cars for you, your boss, customers, and deliveries. Finding a good, clean, reliable company is a process of trial and error. Consider the recommendations of your colleagues locally. Keep a record of the companies you use, with contact names and addresses, and periodically record on a scale of one to ten the quality of service you received. In most cases the individual drivers are self-employed and responsible for their own vehicles; make sure you are using a company that only engages those who keep their vehicles up to a standard you feel will reflect your business. When ordering a rental car in particular, always plan your telephone call; state your requirements clearly and concisely. Always verify the costs, as they can sometimes vary from what you understood they would be.

If you are going to be a regular user, then open an account with your preferred supplier to encourage supplier loyalty. It keeps down cash transactions and accounting entries. When you call an executive taxi for valued customers or clients there can be no embarrassment of them being asked to pay, or you having to pay the driver while the clients stand waiting.

Travel arrangements

Travel arrangements are often a matter of personal preference. Some secretaries prefer to directly book flights and hotels; others prefer to use a travel agent for all travel requirements. In our surveys of professional secretaries, a good, reliable and accredited travel agent has the advantages of flexibility and identifying alternatives in the marketplace. You will pay a slight premium for travel agents' services, but if your boss is a frequent traveler, you will often be able to negotiate compensating discounts. Loyalty to your supplier will pay off in terms of service and quality; and the agents will offer you personally competitive rates for your own travel, vacations, and so on. Any discounts or perks awarded to you must be disclosed to your boss, but few bosses would object to you taking such offers provided they are sure you have not been won over by bribes to an expensive or inappropriate service. Of course your own integrity is on display here; your decisions must be made in the interests of your boss and the firm for whom you work.

Keep a detailed record of your boss's favorite airlines, routes, hotels, and other travel arrangements to ease your ordering requirements. Ask your local travel agent to keep you updated on promotions and incentives, such as air miles, if your boss is a frequent traveler.

Dealing with subcontractors

You and your boss cannot possibly do everything, and for busy periods you may have to subcontract work to third parties. Your firm may be one where subcontracting is normal; the building industry, for example. If this is the case, you will have to administer payments to them and, possibly, monitor their work.

It is essential at the outset to put your subcontractors on a professional footing. If the subcontractors are ruled to be employees, then your firm may be liable for taxes that you may not have deducted from payments made to them. Before taking on subcontractors, take advice from your accountant. If your subcontractor cannot show you the documentation these advisors demand, then always deduct the correct taxes. Your firm is responsible for correct deductions and you can always refund your subcontractor if it turns out that it is entitled to be paid gross. Pay your contractors by check if you can. If a cash arrangement has been agreed on, always get them to sign a receipt for cash on a preprinted form of your design and origination.

Remember your own professional standards: do not take presents or any form of reward (yes—bribe!) for giving them work. Some small gifts, say at Christmas, are normal and genuinely offered but remember to share them with your boss, or at least disclose them to him. Keep your relationships with contractors at arm's length: it is very difficult to have a professional working relationship with people you are too close to. You can be open to pressure to use them when you might want to use alternatives.

Keep detailed records of all transactions with your subcontractors: whom they have worked for, what jobs you have used them for, and some objective comments on their performance. Subcontractors represent your firm as much as your boss and you do, and you are therefore entitled to insist on a reasonable dress code, politeness to customers, quality, and timely work. Make sure that you or your boss regularly visit contractors on-site.

Subcontractors are invaluable for busy periods and are of course less expensive than taking on your own staff, but in the long run there is no substitute for your own trained and motivated people.

Company credit card

Encourage your boss to take out, through your bank, a company credit card. It is a very useful tool to keep track of expenses incurred by your boss. Agree that your boss will only use it for company expenditure; this will help both of you to keep company and private expenses apart. Each month you will receive a detailed statement of expenditure, which can be matched to the transaction slips that your boss should give you weekly. Any transactions that you do not agree with, discuss with your boss.

Determine with your boss whether you have permission to order goods and services by telephone using the company credit card number. This is very useful for larger transactions such as car rental, travel bookings, hotel bookings, purchases of items such as office equipment, and so on. Special guarantee terms also give your firm some additional protection if the services or goods turn out to be unsatisfactory, and most credit card companies give free insurance coverage for a period of time. Company credit cards have to be paid only once a month; this will make your accounting life easier, as well as keeping down your bank charges.

Training

You and your boss are an important team and one of the team maintenance needs is training. The Lone Arranger should take responsibility for the training needs and procurement of both of you. Working for yourselves, it is all too easy to forget your training needs, and only concentrate on skills training as and when the need arises. You should agree on a training plan and a budget with your boss. The training plan should separate skills training from development training and list possible training providers, with a brief outline of the courses together with the cost.

Skills training is about being efficient and getting the job done. Skills training will include how to work a computer, or a new computer program, export documentation, bookkeeping, and so on.

Development training is about being effective and developing yourself and the business. Development training will include interpersonal skills such as negotiations, presentations, sales development, and general management training, as well as developing more products and services and managing people such as subcontractors.

When compiling your training plan, you can obtain help from trade associations, your own professional secretarial association, local colleges, and government-funded training bodies. It is a good idea to network with fellow secretaries to see what training they are undertaking. Keep up-to-date with necessary professional journals and highlight what you think is interesting as well as essential for you and your boss. Funds permitting, do not always restrict training to what is essential now, but consider forward opportunities too.

Physical communications

As the hub of the firm, you will be responsible for the communication strategy and network. The network will be between you and your boss, you and your customers, suppliers, banks, and so on, and between them and your boss. Regarding strategy and equipment there are many alternatives. Your communications setup will also be influenced by the type of business you are in, which will in turn determine how often you and your boss need to be in touch.

The minimum requirement for a small office is: a one-line, two-extension telephone, a fax, preferably with a separate line, and voice mail. With this arrangement, you may agree that your boss calls you at least twice a day to pick up any messages. Building on this, you might like to get your boss a pager that will work in designated zones. They are not intrusive, as they can be switched to silent mode. Most pagers are numeric, i.e., showing which number to call, but more expensive models have message functions for short messages.

For faster communications, cellular phones are best. They are now relatively inexpensive to purchase and reception has improved from their early days. If your boss travels a great deal by car, consider a hands-free car phone for quick communication. If you want to get really hi-tech, consider an in-car fax machine as well.

Customer care and quality thinking demand fast, clear communications. Develop a strategy with your boss, and remember that it is easy to be flexible and upgrade any system.

Negotiations

All of us get involved in negotiations every day, through the simple process of buying things, ordering supplies, or persuading people to do things for us. You negotiate with your boss when you try to agree on workloads that suit you both and you negotiate with yourself when you decide to take a break during the day. Negotiations are the interchange that goes on between people when they endeavor to reach an agreement on an issue, having started from a different standpoint. Some negotiations are formal, but obviously the vast majority are informal everyday encounters.

In the course of your work, there will be many negotiating opportunities; for instance, negotiating discounts (corporate rates) from hotels, negotiating discounts from suppliers for speedy payment, negotiating a vacation from your boss. Although to many people negotiation skills may seem a high-order task that people have to be trained for, in reality this is only because of the high profile of some negotiations that are given prime time in our media when high-profile people are negotiating on behalf of the country, their organization, or their workforce.

All of us learn our ability to negotiate at a very early age and some people take to it at the outset. Those people who enjoy practicing this skill and thereby become good at it often seek employment in an organization that can satisfy those needs, e.g., a salesman on the road, a bond dealer in the financial markets, or a full-time trade union official. For most of us, the development of negotiation skills has to be worked at and needs the application of planning and influencing skills.

First principles

Before we enter into any negotiating position, there are some guidelines we can follow before picking up the phone, writing a letter or memo, or going to a meeting.

It is very important to know in your own mind what exactly it is you want to achieve. This is the overall picture of why you are negotiating a position, and therefore needs to be kept at the front of your mind at all times. If necessary, write it down in large letters so that during the course of the negotiations it will focus your mind on your goals.

Be aware that in the normal course of events, the other party will try to steer you into a different position. You must know what effect their arguments and counter-arguments will have upon you. This can be likened to a mental scale in your head, with minimum and maximum positions that you are prepared to maneuver within.

You must consider whether it is possible to respond to the arguments and negotiating positions of the other party without losing sight of your own goals or giving the appearance that you have backed down. Unfortunately, a lot of negotiators consider it taboo to be flexible because they mistakenly feel that they should not show any sign of weakness, which is often just unfounded obstinacy.

It is a good rule, at the outset of negotiations, to conceal from the other party exactly what you feel the outcomes should be, i.e., not to disclose your minimum or maximum parameters. This will of course enable you to maneuver. For instance, if you are seeking a 15 percent discount from your business travel agent, it is not clever to start the conversation as follows: "Good morning Tim, I've really called to ask you for a 15 percent discount." The better alternative is probably: "Good morning Tim, let me just say how pleased we are with your service. I've just been reviewing how much business we are doing with you and we expect it to increase over the following year."

Skillful negotiators understand bargaining power, and it is important to know what levers you can pull to obtain your goals. As a rule, anything that you have control over gives you leverage. Some examples of leverage are musicians just before a concert, bar staff ten minutes before opening time, and air traffic controllers during the summer vacations. It is important to understand leverage even if you choose not to use it. Leverage must never be exploited, as the idea of sound negotiations is a win–win situation, and use of leverage can often lead to a lose–lose scenario.

Knowing someone, and knowing him well, can be a disadvantage in negotiations. It is always difficult to negotiate with someone you know well and you must ask yourself whether you have the courage of your convictions. If so, do not be afraid to give up short-term popularity merely to prevent short-term disharmony. One of the basic problems here is deciding whose hat you are wearing. Are you negotiating on behalf of your boss, on behalf of your firm, or on behalf of yourself. The rule here is that in any negotiating stance, at the outset declare where you are coming from: for example, if you are negotiating with debtors to collect the firm's monies owed you might open the conversation as follows: "Good afternoon, Tessa, I've been reviewing your account with us and although I have not yet had a chance to talk to my boss on this matter, I thought we could sort something out between us."

The win–win scenario

Successful business negotiations are all about achieving a win–win situation, not a win–lose or a lose–lose. The winning negotiator makes use of all the behavioral skills that we have addressed in the section Assertiveness in Volume 1 of *The Professional Secretary*. To these can be added some simple rules based on other people's successful negotiations.

Aim for a win–win outcome

As we have said, negotiation in business is about win–win. The strategic thinking behind this is that you never know whom you will want or have to do business with again in the future. So it is always worth dealing with people in an open and honest manner, and developing good business relationships with them. A win–lose situation can lead to one party being hurt and seeking some form of redress or comeback in the long run. A few years ago a leading firm of retail jewelers ran into trading difficulties and started putting pressure on its suppliers. It began demanding larger discounts, and insisting that its suppliers held stock until it wanted it. Many of the suppliers had little choice but to go along with this, but the negotiations by the buyers were often arrogant and conducted in a high-handed manner, and a win–lose situation arose. When eventually the jewelry chain ran into severe trouble, many a glass was raised in thanks, and some suppliers started renegotiating with a newly weakened party.

Negotiate in an open manner

Because people are often misled as to the nature of professional negotiations by media coverage and popular myths, a lot of people go into the negotiating room as if they were going to play poker on a Mississippi paddle steamer. We have said that it is not often good policy to open both hands at once, but when serious negotiations are underway, be as open as you can, state your requirements clearly, and encourage openness from the other party.

Act assertively

Assuming that you are certain in your own mind what exactly it is you want to achieve, you have the right to act in an assertive manner. Assertiveness has been examined in Volume 1 of *The Professional Secretary*, but can be summarized as follows.

- always be brief and to the point;
- distinguish opinions from facts;
- express your views in an honest and open manner;
- use "I" statements;
- show you understand what is being said to you;
- suggest solutions where possible;
- ask open-ended questions to encourage other people to have their say;
- listen well and stop talking when appropriate;
- at the end, agree on a course of action.

Avoid exaggeration

Most of us tend to exaggerate what we can or cannot do when we find ourselves in a negotiating position, particularly when we are relating stories to lend emphasis to the point, and invoking what other people have said (e.g., "The boss said . . ."). Exaggeration is great for storytelling but can lead to difficulty if the other party truly believes you, and then quite rightly expects you to act on what you said.

Summarize what has been said

Skillful negotiators see negotiations like a board game, and every now and then you need to stop, consider where you are, and agree with the other party that she must also take stock. For this reason, it is very useful at convenient break points to summarize what has been agreed on so far in order to check for mutual understanding. This process also has the positive benefit of highlighting what has been achieved so far, which will then give impetus to getting the negotiations finished.

Open-ended questions

One of the basic skills of negotiations is the ability to ask open-ended questions, in order to seek information such as opinions and ideas, and gain reactions to such. Open-ended questions are those that cannot be answered with a flat yes or no, often starting off with an invitation to express an opinion or make a suggestion.

Stick to the issue

It is essential to establish in your own mind the issues that need to be addressed rather than getting bogged down in detail, trivia, and criticism. If you are negotiating a pay raise with your boss, one of the issues you may wish to discuss could be the market rate for the job versus your salary. You do not want to be sidetracked into areas of working conditions, and whether or not you enjoy working at the company, which are not the issues under discussion. Make sure that the core issues are established at the outset and, if helpful, summarized so that negotiations can be focused upon them.

Stating unacceptability

If during the course of negotiations something is unacceptable to you, say so. But always take the trouble to explain why you find it unacceptable. For example, if a supplier delivers something late, don't resort to a history lesson of all the times it has happened to you with the supplier and other suppliers, but carefully explain the consequences of the action. Explain that the late delivery will now cause you to be late in execution, and then steer the conversation to the possible courses of action open to both parties to alleviate the situation.

Body language

In face-to-face negotiations, remember your body language and physical presence. Sit beside the other person, or with them if there are more than one. Sit straight, with your head firm but not rigid. Remember to use good and regular eye contact, but don't try to stare someone out. Have a relaxed and open posture and make good use of your smile. Try to make your facial expressions fit the words and the manner in which you are using them, and always look as if you mean what you say.

Payment terms

When you are negotiating payment for goods or services, remember that they are more highly valued before they are performed or delivered than they are afterward. For example, a dentist's bill or quote only looks reasonable when you are in pain. Always discuss with the other party the basis on which you expect to be paid before you do the work or deliver the goods.

When not to negotiate

In order to negotiate well, you have to be strong. There are some circumstances when it is unwise to negotiate, including:

- when you are ill, or depressed;
- when you are in a hurry or meant to be somewhere else, or you are late for an appointment;
- when you are suspicious, bored, or angry with the other party;
- when you are emotionally involved with someone;
- when you are tired, jet-lagged, or hungry;
- when you are desperate, and—more to the point—have shown how desperate you are;
- when you have had the situation sprung upon you at the last minute and you have had no chance to prepare or plan for the negotiation.

Representing your boss

Because you are often negotiating on behalf of your boss, you will find yourself negotiating with other bosses, which as you would expect can have advantages and disadvantages. The advantage of negotiating with other bosses is that, as they are decision makers, you will not have to go through layers of management to get a final decision. They can also offer flexibility in that they can authorize changes and accept offers. The disadvantage is that often once they have made up their minds, there is no appeal against their decisions. Being busy, they are not always on top of things, they do not always believe in equal status ("I'm the boss, you're just the secretary"), so they may talk down to you, and they may be in too much of a hurry for slow-moving negotiations.

Negotiations are a demanding business, and you can find yourself devoting all your energies and attention to getting your immediate objectives. It is, however, a trap to win an argument that cannot be implemented by the other party. Sometimes the third party will agree to something, first to gain a respite or just to get off the hook. For this reason, it is essential to get the other party not only to agree to what you want, but also to agree with you on the feasibility of putting words into successful actions.

Negotiation can be fun and the more you do it the better you will become. Negotiation is an essential part of business communications and the win–win scenario is one in which both parties are relatively happy with the outcome. The Lone Arranger should always be looking for negotiating opportunities to facilitate the working of the business, and for savings that can be made in a professional manner.

Remember that negotiations are all about knowing what you want and using your behavioral skills to obtain the desired outcomes in a win–win situation.

Dealing with Customer Complaints

The Lone Arranger in the workplace is not only a store window but also in charge of running a "one-stop store"; one of your tasks will be to handle customer complaints.

Complaints can come in varying forms, such as letter, fax, or phone call, and they all have to be dealt with in a speedy and efficient manner. Keep in mind that to your customers you are the business, and the way you respond will have an impact upon any future dealings with those customers. Receiving a complaint from whatever source is always an unpleasant experience, even more so when your customer is upset and shouting at you. It produces in you very strong emotions, such as alarm, resentment, and hurt. The natural way to deal with complaints is to defend the business and yourself, and possibly to blame someone else, but normally defensive behavior makes your customer even more annoyed. When customers make complaints, they are normally upset themselves, because they feel let down, and they may have been put into the position of letting someone else down as well. What customers need is a solution to the problem and a demonstration by you of their importance to you, that they are valued, and that the complaint was no fault of theirs.

The problem of "the customer is king"

In many organizations, you can see large posters announcing that "the customer is king" and "customers make paydays possible." But as one person put it, "the supplier is not a doormat." When considering a customer complaint policy, a very useful starting point is to decide exactly the type of business you are in. Let us look at some businesses to clarify our customer response thinking.

Direct consumer sales

Consider a reputable shoe store. In this type of business, the customer is indeed king. Even if a customer wastes an hour of a sales assistant's time and then buys nothing, although the assistant may be thinking, "don't come back for heaven's sake," that assistant will have been trained to say "thank-you," and "hope to see you again soon." In this type of organization, the policy of "customer is king" means that if a customer complains, the store will usually operate a no-quibble money-back guarantee.

The neighborhood bank

In the neighborhood bank, the customer is not quite king. Of course the banks value most of their customers, but they have to deal with them in a professional manner. The bank has to operate within banking laws and act accordingly, and this can lead to many customer complaints, both founded and unfounded. Banks therefore will not operate a no-quibble money-back guarantee policy, but a policy of investigation and report back to the customer with an apology, as appropriate.

The dentist

At the other end of the scale is the dentist. Here you are a customer but the dentist also has a duty of care toward you, and to remind you what you agreed. It is often amusing to be sitting in the dentist's chair being told off gently but firmly that you are not flossing your teeth correctly, although paying for the privilege. Dentists, of course, do not offer money-back settlement for customer complaints, as the risk of a treatment is borne by you.

Figure 7 shows a simple scale that you can use to position your firm.

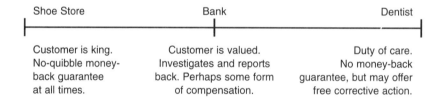

Figure 7 Your attitude toward your customers.

Verbal and nonverbal communication

When you are dealing with complaints, it is necessary to be aware of your verbal and nonverbal communication skills. Use your behavior to win your case.

Be assertive

Being assertive means being honest with yourself and others. It means saying openly what it is you want or need or feel, but not at the expense of your customer.

Listen actively

Listen to what your customer is telling you, show that you are listening, and paraphrase back what your customer said. Show your customer that you understand, and why you understand.

Control your emotions

Always keep your emotions in check and sort your inner dialogue before you reply. Examples of various responses are shown in Table 1.

Table 1 Emotional responses and resultant behaviors.

Customer	Inner dialogue	Feelings	Behavior
Your products are worthless	Who does he think he is	Anger	Aggression
You must have known the product did not work	How could she accuse me of doing that deliberately	Hurt	Nonassertion
Do you normally make mistakes of this nature	I made a stupid mistake, but she has no reason to go on like this	Frustration	Aggression
The job your staff did was second rate and a mess	Shame my staff messed it up; he's getting mad, but I can handle this	Regret Calmness	Assertion

Body language

In face-to-face meetings with customers when dealing with complaints, make sure that you are assertive in your body language to reinforce what you are saying. Look as if you mean what you say, be relaxed, and keep your voice in control. Do not lean forward, and point at your customer; conversely do not look as if you wish the ground would swallow you up. Sit beside your customer. Do not deal with your customer from behind your desk.

Question pitfalls

Use open questions, i.e., questions that can't be answered with a flat yes or no. The wrong way is to say: "I understand that you were not happy with our service" (begging the answer yes or no). The correct way is to say: "I'm sorry to learn that you are not entirely satisfied with the service we gave you."

Ask leading questions, i.e., those that will lead the customer to agree with you. For example, say: "I feel completely taken aback by what has happened, but I know you will agree with me that this is the first time we have ever let you down."

Don't interrogate your customer, don't talk down to your customer, and don't prejudge your customer.

The broken record technique

A very useful tool in communicating with your customer, something that she does not want to hear, is to keep on repeating the basic message until your customer recognizes it. For example, you have got to phone your customer to explain that her car will not be ready until the following morning. "I am truly sorry to tell you that your car will not be ready until tomorrow morning. . . . Yes, I know it must be a disappointment but it won't be possible to complete all the work until tomorrow morning. . . . I'm so sorry you feel that way, but I'm afraid there is no way your car can be ready before tomorrow morning."

Let your customer do the talking

When dealing with complaints face-to-face or over the phone, let your customer do the talking. This will, if necessary, allow your customer to vent frustration or anger. All you have to do is be ready to listen until she has blown off steam, which is the first stage of calming down.

The customer is an asset

For quality products and services, the customer is an appreciating asset. It is your goodwill, so customers need looking after.

The idea that no news is good news does not apply to customer complaints. Just because you are not receiving any complaints does not mean that your customers are happy with your products or services. In Tom Peters's book *Thriving on Chaos*, he makes the point that in a U.S. study, it was demonstrated that 26 out of 27 customers failed to report a bad experience. The reason why they did not complain was that they expected no satisfaction from the company. Another compelling statistic: it was estimated that 91 percent of customers who complained would not come back again, but 82 to 95 percent *would* come back again if their problem was resolved speedily and in a thoughtful manner. Interestingly enough, a well-handled customer complaint usually breeds more loyalty than you had before the incident.

A very useful tool to monitor customer satisfaction is the customer survey. It is almost impossible these days to go into a hotel without being presented with a survey form to fill in. The best customer survey form is one that you tailor-make to the specific needs of your firm, but in Figure 8 we show one that can be amended for your own needs.

Recommendations for a
customer survey form and follow-up

- KISS: keep it short and simple. Keep it to one page.
- Use check-off boxes.
- Reprint your address on the back and prepay the postage for your customer.
- Hand a survey form to every customer at the end of every job.
- Amend the survey form for a twice-yearly survey of all customers on your database.
- Phone or write to customers who do not respond.
- Always reply to customers who do respond.
- Thank them and say how pleased you were to learn of their positive response, or thank them and say how sorry you were to learn of their dissatisfaction, and offer to visit them or invite them to your workplace.
- Once a year, run a promotion with the survey form, e.g., a bottle of champagne for the lucky number.

Dear Customer,

Thank your for being our customer. Please will you be kind enough to check the appropriate boxes in answer to our questions, which we hope will enable us to improve our service to you. No postage is needed and thank-you in anticipation of your cooperation.

Sincerely yours,

APW Training

	Poor	Satisfactory	Good	Very good
1. Was the telephone answered in a prompt and efficient manner when you placed your order?	☐	☐	☐	☐
2. Were you given sufficient explanations of the work to be carried out?	☐	☐	☐	☐
3. Was the work carried out to your satisfaction?	☐	☐	☐	☐
4. Was our staff courteous and helpful?	☐	☐	☐	☐
5. How would you rate the firm's service overall?	☐	☐	☐	☐
	No	Don't know	Maybe	Yes
6. Are we the only supplier of this service to you?	☐	☐	☐	☐
7. Would you recommend us to other people?	☐	☐	☐	☐
8. Will you use us again?	☐	☐	☐	☐
9. Would you like us to visit you or make contact to discuss our services?	☐	☐	☐	☐
10. Can we use you as a reference?	☐	☐	☐	☐

Please write your customer service reference and telephone number here

Comments

Figure 8 Customer survey form.

A ten-point plan for how to deal with customer complaints:

1. Record all complaints, however trivial, in your database. The minimum information you require is: name, date, nature of complaint, action taken, date complaint is resolved, and any follow-up if necessary.
2. Always respond to customer complaints in the first instance by telephone.
3. Respond to all complaints immediately, i.e., that day. If the customer is not available leave a message on his voice mail, send a fax, or mail a letter.
4. Never challenge the customer. Take the view that in the absence of other information, the customer is always right and does not have to prove anything.
5. Do not shift the blame to someone else, e.g., your supplier or your staff. The customer is not interested; and why should your problems be of concern to your customer?
6. When working on a complaint, keep the customer informed. This may well include setting out a timetable for the solution to the problem. Inform customers of delays. In this scenario, bad news is better than no news.
7. Don't promise what you can't deliver. Remember to underpromise and overdeliver; do not overpromise and underdeliver.
8. If you can't sort out the complaint, work to a joint compromise. Make the customer feel that the compromise is his idea.
9. Remember that there are no such animals as minor complaints. In the customer's eyes, they are all elephants.
10. Above all, make sure that your customer is totally happy with the result before you sign off.

Mistakes happen and complaints will occur. Don't get depressed by them. Every complaint is an opportunity to demonstrate your commitment and professionalism to your customer, and that can lead to increased customer loyalty.

We spoke to one building firm that had suffered what its workforce thought was a disaster. While working in a house, they had accidentally unbolted and dropped a very expensive chandelier, destroying it. The boss, obviously a sharp thinker, immediately announced, "This will be a wonderful opportunity for us." The workforce thought he had gone mad! However, he was properly insured, and immediately assured the customer that he would personally attend to a replacement being made (which he did). The customer got a suitable replacement with no difficulty or hassle on her part. That customer now would not use any other builder because she knows that she will be taken care of in the event of problems, and she recommends the firm to anyone needing building work. This is a textbook example of how to make opportunities from disasters.

Customer Focus, and Bringing Quality into Your Firm

Often you will be the sole representative of your firm on a day-to-day basis. The relationship you have with your customers will be the benchmark by which your firm is judged in terms of customer focus and quality of service. There is a common misconception that quality systems and quality matters are the prerogative of large organizations. This is not true.

Who is my customer?

In general terms, a customer is everyone you have dealings with, including your boss, internal customers, i.e., people to whom you are not selling your services but have transactions with (e.g., your bank, insurance company, stationery suppliers), and external customers, i.e., people to whom you are selling.

All work is a process made up of tangible and intangible materials, goods, and/or services. It turns inputs into outputs. Each process we do, however large or small, serves a customer, the person who receives the work we have done. We are supplying our customers with their input to be processed by them in turn. To give an example, if we are sending a sales invoice to one of our external customers, internal customer thinking means that we make sure our invoice is clear, clean, and accurate so that our customer can deal with that invoice (their input) speedily and without queries, so that we can receive our money on the agreed due date. The rule here is that only by supplying products or services that match our customer requirements will we be able to provide them with the wherewithal to do a quality job themselves.

New customer thinking

The basis of new customer thinking is the need to make a profit and to be competitive in the marketplace. In simple accounting terms, profit equals revenue from continuously satisfied customers. If long-term profit is the basis for survival, then it follows that business survival equals satisfied customers. What do we mean then by satisfied customers?

Meeting customers' expectations

In order to meet customer expectations, it is necessary to have a high level of mutual understanding through sound communication with your customer. When your customers talk to you, listen. They will give you free and valuable information about you, your firm, your boss, and your products and services. Meeting customers' expectations also means giving a quality service or providing quality products. Most people have an understanding of quality but find it difficult to define, because the word is misleading as it is so often used as an adjective (e.g., a quality person).

The international standards organization defines quality as: "The totality of features and characteristics of a product or service that bear on its ability to satisfy a stated or implied need." Quality writers have defined quality as conformance to requirements, fitness for purpose, and variance from a nominal or target value. But in the end, it boils down to: is my customer getting what we agreed, and does that match up in the mind of my customer?

An example of the problem of quality thinking is as follows. A few weeks before Christmas you purchase a toy for a nine-year-old. The toy is of the highest quality and was manufactured by a tried and tested company. You wrap the toy up and think no more about it. On Christmas morning, the nine-year-old opens the toy, but is disappointed to learn that there is no battery. You know it is a quality toy. But what does the child think?

Continuously improving your goals and services

Whether you are in the business of providing goods or services, long-term survival means continuously improving your products so that your customers will not go elsewhere. Businesses that do not improve and meet changing customer needs and expectations will eventually go out of business. The starting point for improving is to ask your customers on a regular basis to suggest ways you can improve; after all, they know more about your product and services than anyone else. Remember that unless you have a monopoly in the marketplace, your products and services will have a finite shelf life. The message is improve or bust.

Being very responsive to your customers' needs

Customers change and their businesses change. The problem of monitoring this type of change is that you are so close to your customers that you do not see them changing. It is a little like watching your close friends grow older; you don't notice this, but should you bump into an old friend after a gap of ten years, both of you will notice the changes that have taken place. What we recommend is that at least twice a year you and your boss visit your customers at their workplace and conduct a customer audit. This audit does not have to be too detailed, but sufficient to get a feel for the changes that have taken place. A simple form of audit could read like that in Figure 8, and some of the questions can be answered before the audit.

To the list in Figure 8, you should add your own pertinent questions. The idea is not to spy but to get a feel for your customers' business and to encourage your customers to discuss with you their future plans so that you can take action to meet their changing needs in a proactive, rather than reactive, way.

Being competitive in the marketplace

However loyal your customers are, eventually most will walk if you are charging more than your competitors. A dentist in private practice once told us that if 10 percent of his customers complained about his charges, then he knew he had got it about right. Being competitive means monitoring and tracking what your competitors are charging in the marketplace, and also being in the position of comparing like with like. Unless you can compare comparative quality, the price factor alone will not be significant. We recommend that you build up a database on your major competitors and monitor and discuss all changes with your boss. Being and remaining competitive also means keeping costs down. Being mean and lean is the secret of being flexible in the marketplace.

Customer focus

True customer focus means having empathy with your customer, putting yourself in his shoes. Ask yourself the following questions:

- Would the customer like to work in our office, i.e., is it clean, tidy, visually pleasing, organized?
- Would I buy our own products and services?
- Would I like to be treated in the way that I treat our customers?
- Do our customers tell me exactly what they feel about our business?

True customer focus also means that every action we take, however small, and no matter how far removed it seems from the end customer, takes into consideration the effect of our work upon the ultimate customers, the people who in the long run pay our bills. When focusing on your customer, ask yourself the following for every action you do for a customer:

- Will what I am doing make it easier for my customer?
- Will it help to speed up his work process?
- Will it enable him to do things in a more effective manner?
- Will it make it less expensive for my customer?
- Will it make my customer more profitable?

Remember that customers are won, not born; they may be inherited but they can divorce you and marry someone else.

In order to get true customer focus into the firm, we have to consider some more aspects of quality.

- Quality can only be brought about by positive actions.
- Quality techniques are not enough, however; quality attitude is the key.

Positive actions

Let us first look at what we mean by positive actions. If quality can be described as giving the right goods and services in the right price at the right time, then positive action is doing something about it, if any of the above do not happen. Positive action is not a short-term fix or glossing over things, but thorough investigation getting to the real root cause of the problem. If you supply goods or services that are not quite 100 percent correct, then you must replace the goods or rework the service, or offer a discount in compensation, in order to protect your goodwill. However, this is only a short-term fix. It is very necessary, but the next step must be to take corrective action so that the problem will not happen again. Having taken corrective action, communicate this to your customer.

The corrective action process is:

- Recognize that a problem exists and record it.
- Establish the norm or target, i.e., what should have happened.
- Evaluate and measure what did happen as compared with what should have happened.
- Record the problem, not just the symptoms.
- Identify the causes of the problem.
- Calculate what resources, e.g., time and money or outside help, are needed to solve the problem.
- If possible, come up with more than one possible solution.
- Review with your boss the best course of action.
- Implement the solution.
- Monitor the results, and compare with the norm or target.

Quality attitude

Now we will look at what we mean by quality attitude. Consider whether the following statements are true of you:

	Yes	No
I think mistakes are not OK.		
My customers are the reason I am here.		
I always accept responsibility for the quality of my own work.		
I am honest with my customers.		
I express my commitment through actions.		
I am in control of my work; I do not let outside events manage me.		
I keep my customers advised of any unavoidable delays.		
I seek feedback from my customers.		
Mistakes are avoidable.		
I am proud of the quality of my work.		

If you can answer yes to six or more of these statements, you have a sound and positive attitude to quality. Quality attitude also means insisting on quality in your work and out-of-work life. One of the problems of quality thinking is that if you allow nonquality transactions in your personal life, then you will not be so insistent on quality in your workplace. Let us look at some examples of quality thinking.

- *Wages.* Where society demands it, near total quality is achieved. Wages are a good example. Money is emotive, and employers have long learned to get staff and workforce wages as near 100 percent correct as humanly possible.
- *Electrical appliances.* These days, with total quality control, none of us expect electrical appliances not to work. Is it not irritating, however, to have to buy an adapter and put it on? Is this a good quality attitude by the supplier and retailer?

- *Medical care.* Would you allow yourself to be operated on by a nonquality surgeon, using nonquality surgical instruments and half-trained nurses?
- *Travel.* We are always moaning about traffic and late trains. How can you have a positive frame of mind when you have been delayed for a few hours on a hot dusty day? But the true quality professional has to rise above such discomfort.

Quality may sometimes seem like common sense, but the trouble with common sense is that it is not all that common.

Quality and customer focus have to be worked at. You don't have to like or love all your customers. The quality customer focus approach is simple: treat all customers with the professional respect and duty of care that you like to be shown to yourself. Customers are the lifeblood of your business, and without them you die. A leading writer on quality summed up quality customer focus as follows:

- Nonquality companies overpromise, and then underdeliver.
- Quality companies underpromise, but then overdeliver.

Security and Disaster Planning

As the Lone Arranger, you, with your boss, will be responsible for the day-to-day security of the business. A major aspect of that is to implement a disaster planning policy. In addition, as you may well spend a lot of time on your own, you need to consider your own personal safety. The ever-upward trend in most forms of crime is disturbing. In particular, there has been an increase in white collar and petty crime.

Public attitudes to crime have changed. At present, people are more tolerant of small dishonesty, fiddling has become respectable, and some punishments for white collar crime are a joke. Our police forces are inadequately prepared to handle petty crime, owing to more pressing priorities, and accordingly containment rather than prevention seems to be the current policy. It follows that management and business must now take a large measure of responsibility for crime prevention. This has led some organizations to use outside security organizations to police people movement as well as the protection of documents and equipment. The threats—which are similar for large and small firms—are as follows:

- accidental fire;
- arson;
- out-of-hours break-ins;
- violent crime against property and persons;
- nonviolent crime, including cheating, fraud, industrial espionage.

Without a good security policy, you will not feel safe or be able to obtain competitive insurance coverage for your business.

Security policy

The main aims of a good security policy are prevention, deterrence, and detection.

Prevention

The aims of prevention are to frustrate the planned or opportunistic person who has ideas of committing an offense against you and the business. Prevention is about identifying and anticipating risks to people, buildings, cars, equipment, materials, cash, and so on. More often than not for a small office, prevention is the application of common sense, but if in doubt, you can consult your local police or a private security firm. The following may be helpful:

- Funds permitting, install a closed-circuit television camera to see who is visiting you. At the same time, have an electronically operating door, with a voice intercom, that can only be opened when you press a button to release the lock, having first identified your visitors through the TV monitor and spoken to them through the intercom.
- For ground and lower floor offices, bar the windows or have industrial security glass installed.
- Install a simple security system, i.e., sensors, pressure pads.
- Install window locks.
- Turn your desk toward the door.
- Ask your local fire department to inspect all electrical installations and fire escapes.
- Install a small screwed-down safe for petty cash and important documents.

Deterrence

Deterrence works at a psychological level, warding off a potential threat. Deterrence is the setting up of conditions that make crime—and some accidents—less likely to happen. It is, frankly, about sending the criminal off down the street to someone else rather than letting him try his luck with you. Put up notices: "trespassers will be prosecuted" and "alarm system installed." Use identity checks on visitors. Always switch off all electrical sockets, unplug equipment, and extinguish all smoking materials. Be security alert.

Detection

The objectives of detection are to identify those people or situations likely to allow for crime or accident, and to detect offenses as soon as possible after they have been committed. Some organizations use constant play videos to see who has entered the premises. Detection also includes such devices as smoke alarms.

Personal security

Before the D-Day landings General Montgomery asked soldiers what was the most important thing they owned. Thinking that the general wanted to hear the stock army reply they said, "My rifle, sir." "No," Montgomery would say, "it's your life."

You are responsible for your own personal security. Avoid exposing yourself to unnecessary danger. Adopt the following guidelines.

- Where possible, avoid carrying large amounts of cash. If you have to go to the bank, for example, go with someone. Vary your routine if you are going to collect, or pay in, cash.
- Install adequate lighting outside your office and the building, in the parking lot, for example.
- In very dangerous areas, carry a small personal alarm, and have a panic alarm button under your desk.
- Do not attempt electrical work unless you have been trained.
- Do not attempt to lift heavy machinery or furniture on your own, or when you are alone in the building.
- If you are visiting new customers or meeting someone you do not know, and you will be alone, inform your boss, or at the least a friend, of your movements. Arrange with them a time when you will contact them to let them know you are back safely.
- In an office block or industrial park, try not to be the last person to leave.
- Be alert at all times to your own sense of personal security.
- If you are faced with an incident, put yourself and your well-being before concern for cash, equipment, and documents.

Document security

Every organization has different types of documents, including account books, charts, blueprints, pictures, recordings, videos, and secretarial papers. They all need security. There are many people interested in illegal access to the documents of a successful firm: its competitors, creditors, debtors, investors, and others.

Industrial espionage and other crime aside, fire is the biggest hazard to documents. You will have to decide how sensitive and valuable your documents are, which should be retained and which can be discarded. You must also take into account legal requirements. The law requires certain documents to be retained for a given period of time: account books, bank statements, legal contracts and leases, and so on. Consider the following:

- Destroy source documents that are not required for legal or other reasons. These may include shorthand notebooks, carbon copies, and draft printouts, all of which might be of use to, say, your competitors. Consider how secure your waste disposal methods are. Do you have a shredder? Do you put it in the garbage pail? Do you take it home and burn it?
- Old documents that have to be kept for legal reasons can be a nuisance, taking up valuable space. If space is limited, you may need to consider outside storage companies or a secure lockup.

- Very important documents should be stored in fireproof security cabinets and/or thief-proof security safes.
- Computer disks also need secure and fireproof protection. You should make sure that backups of important computer files are made and stored off-site. Your boss could keep them at her home; you might agree to keep them at your home if your boss requests that.
- When receiving visitors, never leave important documents lying around or on your desk. Most people are very good at reading upside down.

Computer security

Computers need protection from the environment (heat, dust, water), as well as from damage, theft, and fraud. As a Lone Arranger, you might think that you need not be too concerned about passwords, because, if only you and your boss have access, there should be no problems. But even in small offices, sensible precautions should be taken to prevent family, friends, customers, and others from accessing your important information. The best advice we can give is to apply the same security rules that would apply to a larger organization. We recommend the following.

- Locate the computer on a strong and stable platform or desk to avoid accidental damage.
- Protect the computer from the environment when not in use, and apply good housekeeping techniques.
- Install a clean line power supply to avoid surges or fading of electricity.
- Change your passwords frequently. Do not give them out to anyone else unless absolutely necessary. You might need to give them to a temp covering for you for a time; if so, change them when she has left.
- Where temps have to work alone to cover for you, make sure that you remove from the accessible disks on the computer any confidential files, or secure those data areas with passwords you do not give the temp.
- Do not place a computer near pipes, the door, or water facilities.
- Work out in what circumstances you might lose data, and take protective action.
- Back up all important data and store back-up disks in another place.

Disaster planning

Disaster planning is the sensible recognition that disasters can happen. Your job is to make sure that the effect on you, your boss, customers, and others is minimized so that you can be back in business on the same day or as soon as practical. The most common form of disasters today are: fire, water damage, willful damage, accidental damage, and legal closure.

Fire and water damage

Possibly the worst forms of disaster are fire and water damage. These are not only depressing, but often very extensive. In assessing the effect such a disaster would have upon your business, it is useful to have a model of what you would need to keep the business going from another location: an office, your boss's home, or even your own home. You should be insured to cover this, and most insurance companies will make an advance payment to keep you up and running. Assuming that all important documents, in their fire-resistant cabinets and safes, have survived and that you have duplicate copies of your computer disks, then all that is needed in the first instance may well be a new computer and workstation. Most documents can be replaced in time if you request duplicates from your customers, banks, debtors, creditors, insurance company, and others. After the disaster, you will need to establish if the office is still habitable, or how quickly it can be made functional. It will be necessary right at the outset to keep your customers and suppliers informed of what has happened, and to assure them that you have the plans to allow for business as usual. Inform them of temporary telephone numbers, fax numbers, and addresses, where applicable. Don't forget to keep other interested parties informed: banks, and others.

Willful damage

The rule here is: do not overreact; it nearly always looks worse than it is. This type of crime is often opportunistic, not preplanned, and as the thieves do not know what they are looking for, they basically just vandalize the place. In the unfortunate event that you are faced with an incident, stay calm, call the police, dust off the insurance policy, get locks changed, and compile a detailed inventory of what seems to be missing. It is always a good idea to have an office inventory kept up-to-date for use in such emergencies as these, with a copy off-site.

Accidental damage

Accidental damage can have an impact on you and the business, as well as making you or someone else feel guilty. Always make sure that for key equipment you have an all-risks insurance policy. Assuming that a claim can be filed, the only person to be hit in the short term will be "Mr. Cash Flow." When you are auditing your workplace for disaster planning, highlight the key assets that are at risk and make sure that they are individually itemized for your insurance company, so that they can agree with you on exactly what they are at risk for.

Legal closure

Legal closures are on the increase. You need to consider carefully your risk assessment where there are those with the powers to shut you down. Unfortunately there are now many people who have the authority to search your premises and, if something wrong is discovered, fine you, close you down, or make you take corrective action. It is quickly becoming impossible for very small businesses to keep up with all the new regulatory bodies, to track down all the new laws, rules, and regulations that are being enacted. Take advice as often as necessary from the people concerned, such as the fire department, or an independent third party, such as your local chamber of commerce. Other advisors, lawyers, and accountants, for example, can advise on certain specialist areas of risk. The following main authorities can have such an impact upon your business.

The fire department is extremely helpful with advice about fire regulations and preventative measures you must or ought to take. It will warn of any problems and give you time to correct them, only closing you down if your office, building or, say, storage area is so unsafe that you are a menace to yourself and the public. When you move into new premises it is always wise to have the fire department do a preliminary survey.

Banks, building contractors, and other lenders. Providing you are keeping to agreements you signed with them, lenders are not normally a threat. However, it must be recognized that where lenders have security over your property and the assets of the business, they are in a powerful position. If you go over your overdraft limit, your overdraft gets stuck at a fixed level, or you do not keep up with repayments, you may get into difficulty with your lender, who might ask for the loan to be repaid. If you cannot repay or refinance the loan, then the lenders can take steps to recover the money. This could mean your dismissal from the firm if you are to blame for the situation. Discuss any such situations arising with your boss.

Financial regulatory bodies. These mainly relate to the Financial Services Acts, and are applicable to businesses that operate in that area. The regulatory bodies and their powers are currently under review, not least because of the number of financial improprieties they have failed to prevent. If your company is in this particular area of work, and is a member of, for example, FIMBRA or LAUTRO, you can be subject to audits, checks and investigations. Your license to continue business can be suspended or withdrawn.

Health and Safety. Contravention of the health and safety regulations can lead to fines, closure and, in some cases, imprisonment. People may connect health and safety with restaurants and cafés, but the regulations have a great impact on firms involved with potentially dangerous substances (garages, building firms, workshops, etc.). Health and safety representatives can be invited to inspect your premises and make recommendations to your advantage.

Environmental Protection. These agencies monitor and advise on pollution problems. At the moment they are very active with heavy industry, petrochemicals and the like, but the same rules will apply to a small firm running any process that pollutes the atmosphere, ground or water. So watch what you are dumping and putting down the drain; you can be closed down immediately.

Other governmental bodies. The list of these is beginning to look endless, and is growing all the time. Social Security has the right to inspect your salary and wages record, as does Internal Revenue. Your local council may have a noise abatement officer who can seek an injunction to stop you making a noise. The Department of Transportation can inspect your vehicles and, if they are faulty, take them off the road. Planning departments of local councils can put restrictions on your use of property, and even issue compulsory purchase orders to force you to sell your premises to make way for, say, a new road. And so on *ad infinitum.*

In conclusion

As society gets more complex, it creates more rules for the governance of the people as well as industry and commerce. Make it your policy to read a quality newspaper and your trade publications to give you the maximum chance of keeping fully up-to-date.

Decision Making

One of the advantages of being a secretary who is virtually running the office alone is that you will have to be consulted in most, if not all, of the decisions concerning the company. In due course, no doubt, you will have earned the right to make all the day-to-day decisions, as well as inputting into the broader decisions that run the business.

A decision is very simply a choice, whereby you form a conclusion about a situation that you find yourself in. This means that you decide on a course of behavior, on what must or what must not be done. Deciding to do nothing falls into this category. It is the point at which your plans, policies, and objectives are translated into concrete actions. In order to make a decision, you must have alternative courses of action; if there were no alternatives, there would be no need for a decision. One of the basic arts of good decision making is to think up alternative courses of action where there appears to be none.

Basically there are two types of decisions:
1. *Tactical.* These are routine and usually contain few alternatives. In the office context, they usually relate to the economic use of resources. Examples are what type of office stationery to purchase and when to pay the bills.
2. *Strategic.* These are managerial decisions, and involve either finding out what the situation is or changing it, finding out what the resources are or what they should be. The decisions are based upon how the business should be run to make it efficient, profitable, and satisfying of the needs of your customers. Examples are what computer system to purchase and where the office should be located.

Decision making is a process that can initially be summarized as follows.
1. *Generic or exception.* The first step is to evaluate whether the problem facing you is frequent or a one-time-only incident. Frequent situations should be dealt with through a rule or principle that will automatically deal with future recurrences. One-time-only incidents can only be handled as and when they arise.
2. *The boundary conditions.* The second step in the decision process is to understand fully what the decision has to accomplish. What are the objectives the decision has to reach? What are the minimum goals it has to attain? What are the conditions it has to satisfy? An effective decision needs to satisfy the boundary conditions. The more concisely and clearly boundary conditions are stated, the greater the likelihood that the decision will be an effective one, and will accomplish what it set out to do. Conversely, any serious shortfall in defining these

boundary conditions is almost certain to make a decision ineffectual, no matter how clever it may seem at the time.

3. *What is right versus what is acceptable.* You will find it necessary to think through what is right, i.e., the solution that will fully satisfy the specifications, and then give attention to compromise and concessions needed to make the decision acceptable. If you do not know what is right to satisfy the specifications and boundary conditions, you cannot distinguish between the right compromise and the wrong compromise.

4. *Decision into action.* The next step is to build into the decision the actions necessary to carry it out. If thinking through the boundary conditions is the most difficult step in decision making, converting the decisions into effective action is normally the most time-consuming one. But a decision will not become effective unless the action commitments have been built into the decision from the start. In fact, no real decision has been made unless how to carry it out in specific steps has been recorded and implemented.

5. *Built-in feedback.* Finally, a sensible feedback system has to be built into the decision, to allow you to check what actually happens against what you expected to happen. The greater the availability of warning signals about your decision, the more confidence you will have in taking quick and timely corrective action.

A decision is only a judgment made at a particular time with the information you had on hand. All people are fallible and at their best their works do not last long. Even the best of decisions has a probability of being wrong, and even the most effective decisions eventually become obsolete.

Is action really necessary? The alternative of doing nothing is always available. A decision is often an intervention into an existing way of doing something, and therefore carries with it the risk of shock. Do not make unnecessary decisions; the popular phrase is "don't fix it unless it's broken." You only make a decision to change something when the existing condition is likely to degenerate if nothing different is done. There is no formula for a right decision, but consider the following guidelines:

- act if, on balance, the benefits greatly outweigh cost and risk;
- act or do not act, but never hedge or hesitate.

The decision is now ready to be made. The specifications have been thought through, the alternatives explored, the risks and gains weighed. Everything is known. It is at this point that most decisions are lost. It becomes suddenly obvious that the decision is not going to be pleasant. It becomes clear that a decision requires courage as much as it requires judgment. Do not give in to your own demand for reflection. If you believe that the decision is right and will be effective, take it.

Exercise 4: Decision questionnaire
Will this decision

	Yes	No
Generate more income?		
Increase my productivity?		
Improve quality?		
Utilize my personal skills?		
Make better use of my equipment?		
Reduce costs?		
Reduce waste?		
Improve my morale?		
Improve customer satisfaction?		
Improve my boss's morale?		
Make my boss's like easier?		
Justify the cost?		

If you have more than seven yes checks: do it!

Self-motivation

At its simplest, motivation is what makes people do things. It follows that self-motivation is what makes us, as individuals, do things and what determines the effort we put into the things we do. Things that motivate us can be extrinsic: they come from outside the person. Examples are salary, working conditions, status, and job security. Other factors that motivate us are intrinsic: they come from inside the person. Examples are type of work, responsibility, sense of achievement, and personal growth.

Because the Lone Arranger works virtually on her own, the ability to self-motivate is of prime importance. As a Lone Arranger, you have a duty to yourself to provide the best extrinsic factors possible; by negotiation with your boss, you will have agreed on such factors as salary and working conditions. However, by virtue of the job you have chosen to do, the intrinsic factors are equally, if not more, important to you. You must be concerned with the nature of your work, taking responsibility, satisfying your need for personal achievement, and personal growth. In other words, you have taken control of the whole job rather than working in a team situation where it is possible to share and delegate. You must have the determination to approach your work with a positive attitude.

You can improve and sustain your self-motivation by developing a positive way of looking at situations. It is particularly important for the Lone Arranger to take personal care of self-motivation because on a daily basis there will be no one to interact with in a motivational sense. Note the differences between a positive and a negative approach. A positive approach embraces learning and using constructive attitudes and habits, and adopting creative and flexible thinking. A negative approach includes applying destructive attitudes and habits, and working with unimaginative and rigid thinking.

Under the following headings, we provide a practical guide to how to treat yourself as the person responsible for your own self-motivation.

Self-audit

In order to develop and nurture a strong belief in yourself, at least semiannually write down a list of all the things that you are good at. In particular, list areas where you have been told you excel. A review of these will lead to an inner confidence, which in turn will remove the "I can't" from your thinking and replace it with "I am more than capable of doing that."

Try your hand

Take the view that you are almost always capable of more than you believe. Refuse to limit yourself by hanging on to old assumptions about what your potential is. Let yourself go, and try your hand; you will be pleasantly surprised at what you can do.

Positive thoughts

Practice thinking positive thoughts. It is all too easy to become cynical and suspicious about your own, and other people's, motives. Remember the old saying, "Consider your glass half full, instead of half empty."

Be successful

Desire success more than you fear failure. If you don't give it a try, nothing will change or improve. Possibly things will not get any worse, but they certainly won't get any better either.

Achievement

Be a self-achiever. Self-motivation is about having a very clear idea of what you want to achieve, and being determined to get there. The clearer the goal or objective, the easier it is to be self-motivated.

Do it now

Do it now and do it right. It is tempting to put off to a later date things you do not want to do, especially unpleasant things. But if you concentrate only on happy tasks, eventually the "don't-want-to-do list" will be so large that your self-motivation will decrease.

Take control

Take control of your life and your job. Make sure that you are always in control of yourself and the situation. If you are to be controlled by someone else or a situation, make sure you know why you have allowed this to happen, and then you can still be positive in your approach.

Problems

Problems arise daily, weekly, and monthly, and the Lone Arranger might not have someone to share them with. Never dwell on current problems or potential ones. If you are able to do something about a problem now, sort it out right away. If you can't, learn to realize that there is nothing to be gained by worrying about it. Don't cause yourself stress by thinking about problems that may never happen.

Managing situations

Being virtually on your own means that you will be exposed to more situations and experiences than your colleagues in larger organizations. Regard every situation and experience as a learning curve. You can learn from both good and bad experiences and at the least you can always carry away something useful by learning about yourself and others. By reviewing the situation, you can learn why it happened, so that you are in a better position to avoid a similar occurrence in the future.

Accountability

Working on your own means that you are responsible and accountable for your own actions. Therefore, the saying "never pass the buck" in your case is often changed into "you can't pass the buck." This inability to blame others or to criticize or complain can be very frustrating. So why not tell yourself off, saying to yourself that you made a stupid decision, or did a strange thing in the circumstances? If you are feeling very wound up about a particular issue, write a letter of complaint to yourself. This is a good safety valve, and it is very self-motivational for you to realize that you can be professionally objective about yourself.

Coach yourself

You are on your own, with no one to praise you or to counsel you. Be your own coach, give yourself a quarterly appraisal, obviously involve your boss if you can, but more importantly review your quarter as objectively as you can. Construct your own appraisal sheet. Recognize yourself and reward yourself.

Enthusiasm

Enthusiasm breeds enthusiasm, but when you are on your own it is difficult to be enthusiastic, as enthusiasm was made to be shared. Every day find things to be enthusiastic about in your life and your work. Share it when you can; phone someone and tell her.

Live in the present

Make sure you get the most out of every moment of your time. Always be honest with yourself that if you are not using your time at work and home effectively, it's due to you.

Honesty

Learn to deal honestly with yourself, especially after an upsetting experience. Rather than trying to suppress or ignore your feelings, let them run inside you. Remember that you are entitled to your feelings. Don't break down or lash out at other people or things; the most positive response is to allow yourself to talk through your feelings by taking time out temporarily. Switch into doing something different, e.g., take a walk, phone a friend, or arrange to have a talk with someone.

Wrong decisions

When, as we all do, you make a wrong decision, or make a bad deal with a customer or supplier, always put it into perspective. Try to imagine the big picture and don't get bogged down in trivia or detail. Because of the number of tasks we do, often something will go wrong. Consider what percentage of the whole picture they make up. The secret is not to overreact. Ask yourself some basic questions. Just how important is it in the long run? How could it have been worse? How will I view this in a few weeks time? What can I do now to help the situation?

Getting stale

Working on your own or with a very few contacts can be difficult over a period of time, in that there is often little opportunity to experiment with new ideas. It is easy to get stale. For this reason, it is a good idea to be your own consultant and efficiency expert. Every six months, allocate some time to examine critically what you do and why you are doing it. Look at the methodology of your work, the equipment you are using, and in particular the output and the quality of your work. Look forward to these six-monthly internal housekeeping sessions and plan for them. Discuss the results with your boss. If necessary, make a mini-presentation to her together with your recommendations for a new piece of equipment or software.

Networking

Working on your own over a period of time can make you very inert. This can lead you to become suspicious of new faces, and your interpersonal skills will suffer. It is essential for the Lone Arranger to network, particularly with other professionals. There are many professional organizations for secretaries that arrange meetings, seminars, training sessions, and courses. Meeting new people in a similar field is challenging, with fresh views and perspectives as well as opportunities on hand.

Conflict

In your professional life, you will sometimes find yourself in conflict. Conflicts can arise with your boss (not too often, we hope), customers, suppliers, or bankers. Self-motivation means acknowledging the good side of conflict. You do not have to be afraid of conflict between yourself and others if you realize that often it leads to better decisions by causing issues to be challenged and looked at more fully. Conflict can encourage change and strengthen relationships if it is handled responsibly.

Ambitions

You must have ambitions that you can realize now. Short-term attainable ambitions are the fuel of self-motivation. They keep you going and are a great source of enjoyment.

Help

"Are you sure you're using all your strength?" said the father to the son, who was chopping wood. "Yes, Dad," he replied. "No you're not," the father said, "because you haven't asked me to help you yet." Self-motivation can only be sustained if you recognize when you need external help, and are not afraid to ask for it, from yourself and from your boss. As with all professional people, there will come a time when your own inner resources are not sufficient to provide you with a clear way forward. Don't be too proud to use others, whether friends or colleagues, as a source of advice or assistance. Remember that your fellow professionals are in the same situation and welcome exchanges of ideas and issues.

PART 4

Motivation, Communication, and Influencing Skills

Whether working alone or in teams, successful secretaries, like all people in business, get things done through other people as much as through themselves. Complex business relationships need good interpersonal skills. In this part of the book, we examine the three principal skills secretaries in our training courses have identified as important: motivating others, communicating, and influencing others.

Motivation

The secretarial team leader is a first-line manager and one of her roles is to motivate the team. But motivation is not restricted to management. We all have responsibility for our own motivation and if the organization is blocking our normal motivation flow, then we have a duty to point this out to the boss or to someone in the organization. At its simplest, motivating people makes it possible for them to do things willingly, so that they put their best efforts into the task at hand. As we shall see later, motivation comes from both internal and external sources, and of course people are motivated by different things and at different times in their lives as their needs change.

We must first examine the theory of motivation; then we can look at the practical ways you can motivate your staff.

You cannot motivate in isolation. You must take into account the economic climate of the business and the culture of the business; these factors will impact on your ability to motivate those around you. The reason why motivation, especially in teams, is becoming so important is that it is often the edge that makes the difference between doing a job well and doing a job excellently. Understanding motivation theory, however, is not enough in itself. The understanding has to be put into practice, using your communication and influencing skills in your interactions with other people. Here we shall be looking at motivation and its relationship with our ability to communicate and influence.

People have many different needs; one of the most important is the need to achieve. People with this need to achieve prefer situations that have moderate risks and in which they can see their own contribution. Such people prefer to receive quick, concrete feedback concerning their performance and are motivated by the need to accomplish challenging tasks. As the tasks become less challenging, they will seek more challenging ones. Some people are driven by the need for power. These people prefer situations in which they can get and maintain control of the means of influencing other people in the organization. They like being in the position of making suggestions and influencing through presentation skills, negotiation skills, influencing skills, and talking other people into doing things. Some people have a major need for affiliation. Such people have a strong desire to maintain close friends and to receive affection from others. They constantly seek to establish and maintain friendly relationships. Obviously these people prefer to work in teams. People are motivated by these needs as they seek to satisfy them and the need—once satisfied— is not there any longer and is no longer a motivator. If you are replete after a meal, you will not be motivated to satisfy hunger, at least not for a few hours.

The needs of the individual in motivation can be classified into lower level needs and higher level needs. Lower level needs are the desire to avoid pain and satisfy the basic needs of existence, such as food, clothing, and shelter. Higher level needs relate to the requirements for psychological growth, including achieving difficult tasks to obtain prestige and to receive recognition. More than one need is normally active at any time; people trying to satisfy lower level needs may well be looking for power or status at the same time.

Money can satisfy several different needs. If you ask most people at work what motivates them, they will usually identify money. But money or reward, which of course can include benefits such as company cars, pensions, and medical health, are only part of the answer. Studies show that on reaching a certain level of income, the majority of people look for other motivational factors, such as recognition for doing a good job, sometimes just a simple "Thank-you, you have done a good job." The job of the team leader as well as the individual members of the team is to recognize not only what motivates the team as a whole but also what motivates the people within the team on an individual basis.

Let's start with the basic idea that money is a prime motivator. Most people go to work for money, mainly because they have to. Given a choice with enough money to satisfy their needs and other requirements, some people might continue to go to work, some probably would retire, whereas others might want to change their job and do something completely different.

So what do we really know about money? Certainly it is the major mechanism for rewarding people at work. However, very little is really known about how it works, as people have many different ideas of how money is important to them. There is also a cultural bias to take into consideration. In most Western countries, there is a conflicting belief that money is bad (profits are bad) but what it buys is good. In some countries, money is regarded as good: the more you get the more status you will have in that society; your God is smiling on you. Unfortunately, money has also become the basis of comparison in our society. People are all too often judged by what they are earning rather than by what they are doing. This can have very unusual and disturbing effects on the way we reward people in our society, which market forces alone cannot always explain. We reward teachers and nurses with so little and rock stars and tennis players with so much. Furthermore, rock stars and tennis players are allowed to be "bad," but we expect our teachers and nurses to be "good." So differing forms of status come into the equation; in some cases poorly paid people with high status, such as clergymen, can be compared with highly paid people with a lower status, such as some politicians.

Money is also the basis for reinforcement in our business society. We reward people by money and we punish people by withholding money. If you do a good job, you may get a bonus, but for those colleagues who do not, it can be a very punishing experience, not because at this point the actual cash is important but because someone has been singled out as being unworthy. In one large organization that we have been working in, after quite a few lean years, it was decided to pay a flat bonus to all members of the business. But some of the people in the business did not deserve a bonus, and were told so, so there was the very bizarre situation of people being called in by their boss to be told, on the one hand, the good news that they would receive the same bonus as everyone else but, on the other hand, that they didn't really deserve it. This was not particularly motivating for the receivers.

Money is becoming a hedge against job insecurity. The threat of unemployment today is greater than in the great depression of the 1930s and money has become much more important as a protection against losing the job. In most of the organizations that we work for, it is very depressing to talk to so many young managers and staff whose total preoccupation is calculating when they can retire without having to get another job to survive. Long-term job security is a thing of the past; people must constantly earn their right to their job. This means that as and when the opportunity arises, people will maximize their earnings and bonuses in relatively short periods of time, not necessarily out of greed but to save up for the "awful" day when they are dismissed.

The threat of unemployment impacts on us for reasons other than money. The threat of losing your job also raises doubts about what the next job will look like. For instance, if you have to take another job, will it be as challenging as the job you do now? What variety of tasks will it entail? Will you be able to continue using your skills? What is the status of the job? Will you be able to develop personally in that role, and make decisions?

What, then, is the basis of reward for secretaries in the modern business organization and the basis of reward for the secretarial team? This is more complicated than it looks and depends on the size of the business, how profitable the business is, what the market share is, and the prospects for the business in the long run.

In the 1960s and 1970s, the secretarial salary was determined by supply and demand in the marketplace. Employment agencies at that time could virtually dictate what employers should pay. In the major cities, where the secretarial agencies had the most direct impact, they would advise employers of the going rate for a range of secretarial skills, such as shorthand typist, longhand typist, varying typing speeds, and ability to use machines in the office. Information technology has tended to even these things out so that the rate for the job is now more determined by what the business does, and by what other people are earning in the business, and in some cases the status of the boss for whom the secretary works. A secretary working for the chairperson or chief executive of a corporation will normally earn more than the secretary of a project team with, say, five professional staff to look after. In this example, there might be no particular difference in secretarial skills, and the remuneration of a professional secretary is now very much more akin to that of managers in general, based on status, performance, and the performance of the business.

Our conclusion is that money is a prime motivator. Perhaps more clearly, a lack of money is a prime demotivator. If you pay a professional secretary well, she may be productive and efficient, more so than if she felt underpaid, but there is no evidence that a high rate of pay will necessarily lead to a more motivated secretary. What we do know is that fair pay and good working conditions will encourage people to stay longer in your organization.

We also know that money satisfies the basic needs of the individual. With money, you can purchase the variety of goods and services that you, on your own, or with your partner and friends, have decided that you need for your particular lifestyle. But once you have reached a certain level of income, other motivational forces will come into play. The problem here is that it is often difficult to decide the level of income that sparks off the next motivation. Person A may well decide that survival means a semidetached house, a car less than four years old, a two-week vacation abroad, and a basket of consumer goods including a VCR and television. Person B may have decided that a small rented apartment with a minimal number of consumer goods and a bicycle to go to work on is sufficient for him. So, even if we can't accurately define the income level, we can generalize and say that at different points in the money reward system, people will want something else from their jobs and will be motivated to seek it. And having sought it, if they can't find it, demotivation may arise. If it is found, they will be more motivated than if they had been denied it.

According to the psychologist Abraham Maslow, the next stage of motivation is the need for security, in particular job security. When Maslow was writing, job security was readily available in most of the large organizations and people motivated by job security would join those type of businesses, such as civil service, the post office, or public utilities. The move to a market forces economy and privatization has meant that very few people now have job security, which, as we stated above, means that people are seeking to replace that security with more money put aside for a rainy day. Employers have become willing to trade off salary against job security.

Motivating people by using incentives is probably the most common form of lever used by management and can be applied to teams as well. But incentives need constant review, because in due course, their effect will wear off.

Let us look at the case study of Andrea. Andrea left school at age 16 with very few formal qualifications and eventually, after trying a few jobs, went into the travel agency business. After learning her trade in a large organization, she found a small family-run firm and now heads up a small unit specializing in business travel for local businessmen. Andrea's salary is relatively low, probably about half what a professional secretary could earn in a major city, but she receives a small bonus at Christmas if the business has done well. Andrea is now an expert on business travel. She is diligent and has excellent customer care skills. What motivates Andrea? The answer—as near as we can discover it from our discussions with her—is the challenge of the job, i.e., matching customers' requirements against the schedules and routings so that they can get to their destinations. Another motivation is the perks: she gets free trips to very interesting and exotic places all over the world at least two to three times a year, as well as other jaunts up and down the country. Money, then, cannot be the prime motivator here although it can be argued that with a much higher salary, Andrea could possibly afford to purchase the travel perks that she now receives free. But she enjoys traveling and staying at the best hotels, with the added status of being in the business and being one of the select club, i.e., a travel expert. Andrea's job also offers a higher degree of job security than is normal for that type of business. Andrea is therefore one of those people who are motivated by incentives. Her rewards, and travel prizes, are linked to her performance. Many people have this form of motivational drive and if necessary will increase their effort to get the desired reward. However, the reward has to be worth it in her mind. No doubt if the only incentive open to her was a trip to Hong Kong, then after the fourth or fifth visit to that place, the motivation to get that reward would start to diminish and the business would have to put a different venue on the menu in order to keep Andrea's motivation intact.

Some studies, have demonstrated that there are factors controlled by the organization that would not motivate you even if they were very, very good, but would demotivate you if they were bad or were perceived to be bad. These include company policy and administration, supervision, your relationship with your boss, working conditions, salary, your relationship with your colleagues, your personal life, your relationship with your subordinates, your job status, and job security. As long as they are fair, i.e., they are perceived to be as good as the next person's or indeed the next company's, they will not necessarily demotivate you or motivate you.

Psychologists also looked at the effect of intrinsic motivational factors, i.e., influences that come from within you and thereby motivate you to do the job as well as you can. These intrinsic factors include achievement, being recognized for good work, the job itself giving responsibility, prospects of advancement and personal development. People with very high intrinsic needs will seek out jobs that fulfill them and if they cannot find them in an organization they will normally end up working for themselves or in small groups. Therefore, in order to motivate people, we must begin to build these intrinsic factors into our jobs.

It is certainly time to reconsider the traditional theories of motivation and how they can apply to the present business society we live in. We are in no doubt that the way forward in motivational thinking is the acknowledgment that we are now having to deal with a different type of workforce. The new staff members coming into our organizations have a different view of our economic and social systems from people, say, twenty years ago. The role models of integrity, efficiency, and reward for hard work are few and hard to find. Business leaders are not setting a very good example of how to conduct corporate affairs; the recent spate of huge salary increases for chief executive officers is having an adverse effect on their individual ability to motivate and lead their companies. Modern staff members are typically well educated, well read, and well informed. They are used to challenging the accepted in their schools and asking the question: why? Businesses are having to change their traditional ways of dealing with these people. They are moving from a culture of control in the workplace to a more empowered way of working, with a more customer-focused organization as they realize that customers have a choice and can and will vote with their feet.

How can we motivate the modern staff member? One starting point is to make sure that we put a company culture in place that encourages both motivational and personal development for the individual. This can be done through training, and in particular the development of interpersonal skills such as presentation, communication, influencing skills, and negotiation skills. This will build the staff's confidence in challenging the work (i.e., the way they do their work, the vision of the company, and the vision of the teams) and enhance their ability to communicate at all levels in the organization. In this new type of culture, or the way we live with each other in business, we shall be building a climate of recognition. The saying is "what gets recognized gets done." In order to motivate our staff to maintain their degree of professionalism and commitment to the workplace, we will need to define clearly the type of working environment that best suits them, as well as being acceptable to the organization.

Practical motivational forces that you can influence

In the past there was a strong emphasis on Herzberg's extrinsic factors, with the general view being that a happy staff is a structured staff. Too much money and effort was put into working conditions with rigid personnel structures, rules and regulations, and the building of prestigious offices in glass cathedrals. Working in a marble palace is no substitute for boredom and job insecurity. So what type of culture or climate of work are people really looking for? Here we can only generalize from the work that we have been doing in client organizations, but the following might be the basis for the new type of culture that people would like to live in.

Empowerment

People are motivated by empowerment, although empowerment is not as popular as a concept as it was a few years ago. Empowerment is about people taking responsibility for their own actions and making use of the skills they have for the benefit of the organization as well as for their own personal growth. In order to empower people, you will have to give them clearly defined goals with your support. They must have jobs that they have been trained to do and are motivated to do. When empowering, remember that people are not puppets.

Being effective

People are highly motivated by being effective. For too long in business, we have only concentrated on people being efficient. Being efficient is doing the job well with the training and tools you have been given. It also means following the rule book and doing what you were told. Being effective is different. Being effective is challenging the work systems and asking "why are we doing the job this way," or indeed "why are we doing it at all?" Being effective means using your hands and your brain to make the best use of yourself for the benefit of your team and the organization. Encourage the people around you to challenge constructively ways of doing tasks, and to find better and more productive ways. Lead by example: start by a few challenging thoughts today.

Teamworking

Businesses are developing not only self-managing teams but also self-motivating teams. People motivate each other more quickly when working in teams because they communicate with each other. Teamworking can be fun, which is also a motivating factor we forget in our organizations. Take the time to think up ways of making work for the people around you fun. It is the aspect of our corporate life that is most in need of creative thought.

Clear vision and goals

People can only be motivated if they think that there is a good chance that effort on their part will lead to their obtaining some desired reward. We have discussed concrete rewards previously but achieving the goal, i.e., winning, is another form of reward. Give people a clear vision and clear goals; this will give them something to aim for and concentrate their energies on. It must be remembered, however, that motivation can only take place if individuals and teams have a reasonably good chance of accomplishing the goals. To combine challenge and a probability of success is a demanding skill; the tasks you set people—or that they set you—must be achievable, but hard to achieve.

Ownership

When people feel that they own something, they are motivated to take better care of it. One of the problems in our organizations is to make sure that people feel they own the part of the business they work in; then they will nurture it. People need to feel not only useful but also affiliated to the business. Working in teams helps to build affiliation to the team and to the people in the team. Giving shares to staff or selling them at preferential prices may help to build a sense of ownership in the business. But it is still necessary for you to motivate your people, through training and leadership, to feel part of the whole. This is best done by open communication and by making the staff part of the decision making process, especially when it comes to setting the goals and the visions of the organization. Make sure that—as always—you lead by example.

Identification and release of talent

Motivation includes expectancy, i.e., expecting something to happen if we act in a certain way. For many secretaries, their present job is the first rung of the hierarchy or even management ladder. For them it is important, and therefore motivational, that the organization identifies them as prospective leaders and is prepared to train them and then release them from their present positions into more managerial posts. From our experience, being blocked in advancement is one of the most serious reasons why secretaries are demotivated. They dislike being categorized as "not being in the promotion club" and on closer investigation it is normally the boss, not the organization, that is in their way.

Changing the motivational climate of an organization is a massive undertaking. Changing the climate of your team is not necessarily such a huge problem. From our experience, you will achieve it most easily by treating people with mutual respect, setting examples that people feel comfortable with and can follow, and training people to use their skills and talents.

Communications

I said it in Hebrew and I said it in Dutch
I said it in German and Greek
But I wholly forgot (and it vexes me much)
that English is what you speak.

(Lewis Carroll, The Hunting of the Snark)

One of the greatest paradoxes of business is why we still have so many problems in actually talking to each other at the workplace, given the amount of time, energy, and money spent on corporate communications, team briefings, and training staff and management to communicate with each other. It is caused partly because interpersonal training—face-to-face communication—is being set aside in the face of information technology systems: telephone, fax, and electronic mail systems. We now think we can successfully communicate without having to meet people face-to-face. In fact, both types of communication are necessary; both are skills to be learned.

The professional secretary is at the hub of the communications wheel, being both the transmitter and receiver of information to and from herself, the boss, and internal and external customers. The secretary's job is to filter communications to make them acceptable. For instance, if the boss calls you in and says, "Tell that lazy so and so Giles to see me before he goes home with that file" you, as the professional secretary, will have to decide how to communicate the message to Giles. You must decide:

- what medium of communication to use (E-mail, phone call, or visit);
- how you will express the message (a word-for-word account or a diplomatic translation);
- what if any prewarnings you may decide to give Giles to prepare himself for the meeting with the boss.

Good two-way communications can only happen if both or all parties are in a frame of mind to convey correct information in an assertive and adult manner. As secretaries, you will always have access to privileged, confidential information about the people you are communicating with. The boss may take the view that he can communicate and be listened to because of his position as boss. You cannot afford such a luxury. Your job is to balance the relationship between yourself, your boss, your team colleagues, and other people in the organization.

Who am I?

Before any communication, you must first decide who you are. In what capacity or role are you communicating?

Your relationship with your boss, from an outsider's point of view, can be very complicated. You have a staff relationship with your boss on some occasions, but you will be an extension of your boss and his authority on other occasions. When you communicate, others must know whether it is you speaking, or your boss through you. In the example given above, it is not you communicating and you will not be empowered to alter the message or put any other interpretation on it. Your job allows for your diplomatic skills in delivery, of course, but you won't, for example, be able to answer questions Giles may have.

This is an example of one-way communication, which can be done verbally or in writing, as no feedback is intended. You may make the decision that it is more effective, or more motivating (or at least less demotivating), to do it one way or another. In other situations, you may well be communicating as a secretarial team leader. Here not only do you get treated as being one of the bosses yourself, you are also empowered by the whole team to communicate. In this instance, you will be able to take questions and make the process a two-way communication. On other occasions as well, you may be communicating as a secretary, i.e., the expert on a particular issue or a piece of work where your opinions and views are important. What you are trying to relate is particular to yourself.

The rule is simple. Before you communicate, resolve in your own mind exactly who you are and, when you are communicating to other people, make it clear in what capacity you are communicating so they will understand who is actually behind the message as opposed to who is speaking.

Why me?

Before any communication, ask yourself: why am I communicating this? Why was it given to me to communicate? What motivated that person to give it to me to deliver?

All too often the credibility of a communication is diminished because the wrong person is asked to deliver it. This can cause unnecessary hurt or loss of face. A staff member might want to hear about a promotion or a pay raise from the boss, and not from her secretary, however popular you are. If you decide that you are not the best person to deliver a communication, then decide who is and talk to your boss about your beliefs.

What is the best method of communicating information?

Unfortunately all too often the best method of communicating information is decided based on past practice in the organization. It is time for a new look to decide how we should be communicating better. Each communication mode should be decided on its own merits, not on a vague history about how it was always done in the past.

Another reason for thought is that there are many more alternative communication methods open to you and the boss. In business, we have become lazy in the way we communicate with our staff. This is even more acute when communicating interoffice and inter-site, i.e., from the center to remote factories and to other locations. There are, however, a few ground rules we can follow.

- Bad news should always be delivered by the appropriate person verbally, with, if necessary, a note of what was said to hand to that person at the end of the interview. The reason for delivering this personally is to give the person a chance to ask questions and to clarify the information you are trying to tell someone. The reason for a written confirmation is that emotion may block out the detail of what was said, and the receiver of the news can read the message again later, and more calmly.
- Good news should also be delivered in this manner; this is highly motivating. However, if the situation demands it—the person is a long way away, for example—the receiver will not be too demotivated to receive a phone call or a fax, because the news is good.
- Good and bad news should never be communicated together. This confuses the issues involved and waters both of them down, thereby diminishing their impact.
- Generally, return a communication in the mode in which it was sent to you, i.e., memo for memo, fax for fax, and phone call for phone call. However, consider the expediency and time saving in telephoning replies to letters or memos. This is the sort of radical rethinking mentioned above.

Trust

Trust is one of the most important issues in successful communications. Lack of trust is one of the greatest barriers to communicating with people.

Communication can only be effective and take place to the satisfaction of both parties if we believe, or at least start out with the premise that we believe, what someone is trying to tell us. If we don't believe it, then not only will we not listen but probably we won't take any action on that communication. A general rule is that all communications start out based on trust and it is only when trust has broken down that the communication barriers come up. Trust or lack of it is normally based on past experiences about what the business has done and what the person delivering the communication is perceived to be.

Perceptions and the reputation of communicators are therefore very important. "Them and us" attitudes between workforce and management get in the way of successful communications. In some organizations, usually the larger ones, management is not trusted purely because it is management. Second-guessing in business has become a popular game and often people come out of meetings saying, "Well I heard that but I wonder what they really meant and what they were really after".

We cannot assume trust and, like respect, it has to be earned. Your job, with your boss, is to establish a basis for trust between yourselves, and then to exhibit to others that you can be trusted. The only way to do so is by doing it. When people have learned to trust you, they will continue to do so unless they have reason to learn not to trust you.

Before you deliver any communication, ask yourself, "Would I believe this and would I take action on it?" If the answer is "no," consider that you might be being used to manipulate others; someone may be trying to preserve his own reputation for trust by letting yours be tarnished. Go back to the person and discuss your beliefs and feelings.

Information withholding

Because information is power, far too many people deliberately withhold information to enhance or maintain the power of their position. This is often a sign of a weak boss.

Many organizations are trying actively to encourage more open communications but unfortunately secrecy is part of our society, and is often encouraged. The ability of management to be open is often a function of the size of the business. In very small organizations of, say, fifty or fewer people, everyone will know each other and will have formed very strong communication networks with each other. But open communication in large organizations is a long and often painful learning experience. This is an issue that managers have difficulties with, but if they openly communicate what they are thinking they will be trusted in the long run. In the short run, we know that communications are often treated with suspicion and the communication may cause more worry to the workforce or members of staff.

The best approach is to communicate what you can in an open manner, in particular to communicate the things that you have decided to do. There is little point in communicating information that you are only thinking about doing unless you feel that the knowledge that you are working on a problem will itself be useful or motivating to others, or because you are deliberately flying a kite, testing the reaction from your staff.

People have a right to be consulted and communicated to, but only after the plan or strategy has been fully thought out by you and your boss. Too often staff feel that information is being withheld from them when the reality is that management (you and your boss, perhaps) just has not worked out what to do. If this is the case, then an honest and open approach is to tell the staff exactly that.

Body language

In face-to-face communications, body language is very important. You can say one thing and by your facial expressions, gestures, or signs, you can obliterate the true meaning and confuse others. Always make sure that your expression fits the words and that your stance and posture are appropriate to what you are talking about. The following is a list of some of the things to avoid.

- Finger jabbing, pointing your finger at someone else. This denotes being aggressive or critical of what others are saying and, in some cases, putting people down.
- Drumming fingers on the desk and tapping your feet. This denotes impatience, being irritated or agitated by what you are listening to. It tells the person that you are not really listening.
- Leaning back in the chair, staring at the ceiling, legs up on your desk. This denotes superiority, not being interested and being totally detached from the communication.
- Crossing your legs and holding your arms tightly. This is a defensive attitude that means you are putting up barriers to what you are hearing.
- Avoiding eye contact. Avoidance usually means that you have something—personal or corporate—to hide.

Language style

There are issues to consider relating to the words we use. Some originate from our need to use certain types of words. For example, some people use words that are too difficult for the other person to understand, words that have a multiple meaning and abstract words that permit a wide variety of personal interpretation. They might do this in order to show off, to display their educational background, or simply to hide the fact that they are unsure of what they are talking about. *Cure*: Remember that the clearer the delivery, the more chance you have of winning people over to your viewpoint.

Others use professional or technical terms that have a unique meaning to a specific department, organization, or field of learning. They might use jargon and slang words that have a special meaning for only a certain number of people. This is often because they want to say, in effect, "I'm in a special club and you are not a member," which is very offensive to others. Such language is of course very acceptable to people "in the same club," where it acts as a bonding mechanism. *Cure*: Before you open your mouth, consider your audience.

Another group of problems in verbal communication can relate to the method that we use. Examples include giving too few or too many details, giving the receiver or the audience no opportunity for feedback, using complicated and very lengthy sentences, hedging and beating around the bush, and being more concerned about style and spelling than meaning. *Cure*: Consider the goal of the communication; to make a certain impact. Be more concerned with the impact than the delivery.

The major skill used in nonverbal communications is observing. Observing is using your eyes and ears to pick up added meaning. To a speaker, a yawn in the audience may indicate boredom. A presenter may see a person staring out of the window. These actions are indicators of a message. The difficulty is that these aspects of communication are based on personal interpretation; it's easy to jump to conclusions. This conclusion could be wrong because of three key factors.

First, people can do the same thing but the meaning can be different. For instance, a yawn in the audience might be from boredom or the result of a night on the town. If you react to that one yawn, you may be ignoring an otherwise highly interested audience. Someone staring out of the window may be daydreaming, or actually thinking out a solution to a work-related problem you have raised in his mind.

Second, people can do different things that mean the same thing. A person might have nothing to do so he might put his head down on the desk. Another person might also feel bored but deal with it by starting some work, i.e., busy work. This could be work he likes to do but that is not really going to contribute to the effectiveness of the organization.

Third, people have the ability to hide their attitudes. We have as individuals learned not to express certain emotions. We have learned through experience that some things should not be said or done. Anger, for example, is one of the emotions that is frequently buried and not openly expressed in a work situation. This leads us to conclude that the nonverbal form of communication is powerful. It enables us to get a message, real or imagined, even when no messages are being sent. If you enter a noisy meeting and suddenly everyone becomes silent, the people in the room are telling you something.

The situation between the receiver of the message and the sender is a key element in the communication equation. No one approach is perfect. Responsibility for the level of understanding has to be accepted by the sender of the message. Your goal, as sender, is to achieve understanding; your major concern has to be that people understand the message. The receivers have to get a message that is meaningful, accurate, understandable, and probably that they can take action from. The speaker has to communicate *to* the receiver, not *at* her.

One of the aspects of communication to consider, then, is being a good listener. We suggest the following guidelines:

- understand other individuals' viewpoints without preconceived ideas;
- check their understanding of what you were saying;
- get to the roots of any disagreement;
- help them think things through;
- encourage suggestions from the audience;
- let them know that you are trying to be fair;
- avoid interrupting other people's conversations unless you have something to contribute and it is important to contribute it at that time;
- show that you regard their thoughts and feelings as very important;
- show that you respect the individual as a person;
- establish mutual confidence with the audience.

Start now

First thing tomorrow morning, start by considering the flow of communications within the area of your responsibility: between you and your boss, you and your customers, and your boss and your customers. Make a list of the barriers to communication that now exist. Decide which of those are the biggest problems, and which might be most costly to your company. Get together with your team or your boss and develop a list of solutions that you will implement immediately. If you have a team, be sure to involve them. Make it fun.

Influencing

Influencing is having an effect on someone so that she does or says something that you want her to. This effect can be mental, moral, or emotional, or a combination of all of these. In this section, we shall be considering some of the more common influencing skills that are used in business and the reasons why influencing skills are becoming more important.

In the course of your work, you probably face many situations that make you feel uncomfortable, anxious, angry, or frustrated with the boss, with customers, or with the organization. If unchecked, this can lead to open or covert conflict. The reason you get upset is that your needs, wants, beliefs, opinions, and attitudes are different from those of other people. Have you experienced any of the following?

- Unreasonable requests from your boss.
- Frustration about the cooperation that you are not getting from another department.
- Having to convey decisions that you know that your team will not like.
- Wanting to disagree with a point of view that a senior member of staff or your boss is forcibly expressing.

- Having to handle an irate individual without losing the business or making promises that are difficult to keep.
- Making an important presentation to a group or your team with very little time to prepare.

One of the main reasons why influencing skills are so important is that the traditional position of power is on the decline. In the past, the boss was the boss and if she gave an instruction, it would normally be carried out for that reason alone. In business organizations today, there is still some residual power in our hierarchies but younger members of staff are not so motivated by just taking orders. They quite rightly want to be consulted, to be part of the decision making process, and to understand the reason why they are doing something. Just giving orders is becoming a thing of the past; the success of the secretary and the secretarial team leader often now hinges on her ability to influence others, i.e., to motivate people to *want* to do something. Correctly influencing someone to do something is more motivational and will give you enhanced individual and group effort.

The basic influencing styles we use in business are persuasion, assertion, visioning, bridging, and moving away.

Persuasion

Persuasion is the most common form of influence we use in business. In this style, we propose ideas and suggestions and ask questions of others in support of our arguments. Often we will present tabled facts to support our point of view and we will counter other people's arguments if they don't agree with us. Persuasion can be a lengthy and sometimes boring process, as anyone who sits in on lengthy meetings will agree. It does, however, get things done and is part of participative management.

Assertion

Assertion skills are discussed fully in Volume 1 of *The Professional Secretary.* Assertion is stating what you want people to do in an honest, open, and adult manner. Part of assertion may be to apply a reward or sanction upon people to persuade them to do what you want. This is done by pointing out the consequences of their actions if they go along a certain path. The purpose of assertion is to create a win–win situation.

Envisioning

Envisioning is a more attractive form of influencing skill. When we envision, we share with people the exciting possibilities of what may happen if we do something. Envisioning entails finding and establishing common ground with the people you are trying to influence so that they will voluntarily and willingly be motivated to the course of action you are recommending. Envisioning often takes longer than persuasion, but the commitment may often be very much greater as they have fully made up their minds to agree to a course of action.

Bridging

Bridging skills bring people together who may not yet be in agreement. It entails listening carefully to what people are telling you so that you can summarize what they have said, thereby showing them that you respect and understand their views. Bridging means being more open, telling people what is going on, and asking for their help in sorting out particular problems or issues. Bridging skills are essential in team meetings where people are trying to persuade each other to different courses of action.

Moving away

The moving away influencing skill is used when it is obvious that to continue discussion is pointless or could lead to aggravation. Moving away is disengaging from the situation and, for instance, recommending that we meet again in, say, an hour when tempers are thawed. Moving away also includes the realization that the will of the meeting or the team is different from yours and that on that particular issue you are not prepared to stand in their way.

The degree of pressure to apply

When we wish to influence someone or a group of people, it is also necessary to decide on what degree of pressure we should use. This will often be determined by the situation we are in, and by how much time we have to resolve the problem or the issue. The type of levers we need to use to influence are a personal choice and the two most common are push and pull styles of influence.

Push

The push style of influence is where you make people do something rather than motivating them to achieve your aim. For the push style of influence, you will use persuasion and logical reasoning to explain why something should be done and you can back this up by offering a reward or threatening punishments. You may be aggressive by using your positional power in the organization or you may be manipulative and nag to get your own way. One of the problems with using a push style is that when people have been made to do something, they will have an expectancy of the outcome. If this expectancy is not fulfilled, they may want some form of revenge.

Pull

The pull style of influence is using your visionary skills to motivate people to want to do something of their own accord rather than pushing them into it. Using a pull style is more attractive and normally people will be more committed to the resolution, as they have been consulted and able to think through the situation and make up their own minds. But a pull style of influence is a slower process and it will always be necessary to weigh the urgency and the impact of the situation.

In considering push and pull styles, we must consider the order in which we use them. When influencing people, you cannot use a push style and then move to a pull style if it doesn't work. Your credibility would probably then be suspect. The only way in which you can use both styles legitimately is to start off with a visionary pull style and, if that doesn't work and the situation demands it, start exerting more pressure by using a push style of, say, reasoned argument. As pressure for action becomes more demanding, you might have to move from rewards to punishments in order to get your own way.

We can use the example of meeting deadlines in two scenarios.

Scenario 1

Let's imagine that you are due to deliver a report to a department within ten days. You fail to meet the deadline. After, say, eleven or twelve days, you receive a written warning from your boss, the first notification of any demand. How do you react? If, on the following day, that department's head telephones you and starts using a visionary and bridging style of influencing you, explaining how desperately he needs the report, you might be sympathetic but you will no doubt be upset and angry that you have received a warning after being only two days late, which may well have been an unnecessary use of pressure.

Scenario 2

If, on the eleventh day, the department head telephones you and explains, with vision and bridging, the effect the late report is having upon his organization, you will be better disposed toward him. You are more likely to want to help by reprioritizing the work. No doubt if you continue not to deliver, then you will not be too upset when he starts to exert more pressure, using memos or telephone calls, even to the point of threatening a written warning. (Of course, no one who has read this far through the two volumes of *The Professional Secretary* could ever have got into such a position!)

The decision to use a push or pull style is a matter of judgment and sometimes the judgment has to be reasonably quick. If the building is burning, it is quite in order for you to use a push style of influence and say to your team and colleagues, "Get out of here now!" The alternative of using a pull style would be to sit in the room with flames around you while you create a vision for your staff of what would happen if you stayed in the room, taking your time to move them toward wanting to comply with your request. In this situation, you can see there is no choice: the push style is the only proper course of action.

Damage control

If you have to use a push style, perhaps to meet a sudden and very urgent deadline, remember to limit the damage afterward by explaining why it was necessary. Make it clear that it is not the way you usually work, but that there were extreme circumstances.

Consider the following analogy. We hope you do not make a habit of going around the office physically pushing people around, but if you saw a large, heavy object about to fall on someone you might well push her out of its path. What then? Even though it is obvious to you, her, and everyone else that what you did was exceptional and necessary, even laudable, you would still apologize ("Sorry about that, are you all right?") to make clear the exception. She would of course acknowledge your actions and your concern ("I'm fine and thanks for being so alert"). The balance is restored; you have both established that it is not your habit, and that it has not given you permission to do it again when not necessary.

Situation influence

In order to influence people, it is necessary that you are in the correct frame of mind, as otherwise your thinking process may be faulty. Situation influence is based on the idea that every situation you are in sparks off a thinking process. This in turn draws from your personal feelings about the situation and the people involved in it. This in turn leads to your behavior, the part of you that becomes visible.

All situations are unique, but in order to cope with each new situation the mind recalls all the information necessary to deal with it and the new unique situation. Without this recall factor, you could not form a plan. The mind therefore examines the nearest parallel to the situation that it can. Because the situation is unique, the parallel will not be perfect: there will be flaws in your feelings that may lead you to handle the situation in the wrong way. The point is that your feelings don't arise out of thin air but as part of a process compiled by your mind to cope with the situation. Your past experiences are what really matter here.

The secret of influencing for effect is to get total control of your feelings, not to stifle them but to let them flow through your mind and then to start removing the negative feelings that may hinder your ability to influence the situation correctly. Count from one to ten before engaging your mouth to give you a chance to listen, analyze, and then give your considered reply.

An example of the above was related to one of the authors during an influencing skills seminar. A person had recently purchased a BMW automatic with a powerful engine. Very soon thereafter, he was at a set of traffic lights when an old car pulled up alongside. According to our informant, the driver of the other car looked at him and, grinning, started gunning his engine. The driver of the other car was in his early twenties, whereas our delegate was in his mid-forties. What happened next was that our informant moved his automatic gear lever to the override position for a quick getaway. This was an instant behavioral reaction to his feelings. What was going on in his mind was that there was no way that the other driver was going to "burn him off." Apparently it took him a second or so to realize he was being childish, and he moved his gear lever back to the drive position. He had overridden his negative feelings, realizing that to race the other car in a crowded London street would be both foolish and dangerous. What had happened was that this situation was unique but his mind had reacted the nearest parallel to it, which was racing cars away from traffic lights when he was a teenager on the Southend arterial road. At that time, he added as an afterthought, the roads weren't so dangerous.

Influencing for criticism

In order to grow and advance, the individual, and teams, must be prepared both to give and to receive criticism. But there is a considerable difference between constructive criticism and destructive criticism. Constructive criticism is being helpful; destructive criticism all too often not only is unhelpful but can destroy the basis of trust between the two parties.

Criticism is using all your influencing skills to point out to people or teams where their behavior, performance, or stand on a particular issue is not what was agreed or expected. We seek praise but have to learn to receive criticism. Depending on your job, you may well find criticism being leveled at you by the boss, customers, colleagues, or other departments. Constructive criticism is an exchange between adult and assertive people to put right something that has gone wrong, looking for a win–win situation.

Learning how to give and receive criticism is not easy. People get very defensive as their feelings get hurt about themselves, their professional abilities, and their teams. Conducted properly, criticism can build the individual and the team. It can reduce conflict and help to build trust. Conducted badly, criticism can cause conflict, destroy trust, and hinder the growth of the individual and the teams.

How to receive criticism

The first step is to forget all the destructive criticism you have received in the past and thereby to try not to be on the defensive.

- While you are receiving criticism, try to be empathetic, i.e., put yourself in your boss's shoes if it is he who is criticizing you and ask yourself: "Why is he criticizing me? Why is he criticizing my work? Why is he criticizing my team's work?"
- Listen to the criticism carefully and paraphrase back what you are hearing, so you are both in agreement as to the nature and substance of the criticism. Ask the critic to explain how and why the criticism arose and to state clearly where your performance differs from what the critic understood as the agreed norm.
- Ask the critic to offer you a solution to the problem or get the critic on your side to help you solve the problem. If necessary, or indeed if it warrants it, offer your solution to the problem and explain how and why the underperformance or whatever arose, so that the critic at least has some background information.
- When you have agreed on a course of action, discuss with the critic any follow-up procedures. Above all, don't deny the criticism, don't try to justify and defend

a situation where you know the criticism is just. Don't hide from the situation, don't argue, and, above all, don't get angry. You don't have to agree or disagree with the criticism but your job is to work out a joint solution with your critic.

■ Finally, look upon the constructive criticism as an opportunity to learn and grow.

How to give criticism

The prime rule here is not to address personal issues, but to concentrate on the work-related issues. You must set aside personalities. Make sure you are in the right mood to give criticism. If not, take action to make sure you are. One senior manager we know always goes for a mile walk before any difficult critical interview.

■ Make sure you have a plan of your criticism, i.e., notes on the issues you want to address. Check that your criticism is specific and not a general and personal attack on the person's behavior and work over the past month or year. Saving up criticism and then totaling it for a particular day is only a form of destructive criticism.

■ Tell the person what the meeting is about and then make your specific criticism, e.g., "I have noticed that you have been late for work on Monday and Wednesday last week and Monday and Wednesday this week." This is preferable to a general attack, e.g., "You are always late for work these days."

■ Now invite a response to your criticism. "Can you please tell me why you are late? Is there something you can tell me about this or possibly something you might want to tell some other person?"

■ Then invite recommended solutions to solve the problems, e.g., "Have you considered getting an earlier train?," or if that is not possible formalize the performance difference, e.g., "I can see why you are late on Mondays and Wednesdays because you have to take your children to school on those days, so why don't we change your working hours on those particular days."

The idea of constructive criticism is to bring the good member of staff and/or team back to the agreed and desired performance level or level of conduct. Good criticism reduces stress for the employee as the sense of wrongdoing (e.g., letting people down) is taken away. The aim is for both parties to get positive results from the interview or the meeting, so never be afraid to introduce praise as well as the starting point of the critical interview. This can often help to relax both parties, which will then facilitate what is to come.

Summary

As we have discussed, effective motivation is the understanding of motivation theories and the application of motivational forces through communication and influencing skills.

We have also seen that despite the many theories of motivation, it is apparent that the organization does not directly motivate an employee, but that the organization can demotivate an employee if certain factors are perceived not to be satisfactory. Employees motivate themselves and your job is to understand and know what motivates your team and the people around you. It is your role to provide a climate within which you and others can motivate yourselves.

Employees need to be more right than they are wrong. It is motivational to communicate to employees how well they are doing, or to put setbacks into the best possible light. Being right creates a "feel good" factor that encourages staff to stretch themselves.

Employees need to know what is going on around them. People fear what they don't understand. We recommend regular team briefing meetings that concentrate on local issues, so that people have a chance to see how they are performing in the context of what is in their control. All employees want to work effectively but in order to do so they must be able to understand and appreciate the problems and needs of the job and to know how they can contribute.

Employees are motivated when the organization helps them to analyze and understand their capacity for growth. Although members of staff will tell you that they are content in their present position, this does not mean that they do not want to grow and be promoted.

Employees are better motivated when they can work to their attainable and agreed goals to achieve the goals and vision of the organization. Employees are motivated by a business doing well, especially when they feel they are making it do well. They need a sense of importance and they need to feel that they are a responsible part of the organization and that their jobs are of value to the organization.

Job motivation includes the introduction of responsibility into routine repetitive tasks. Total quality management in our companies has gone a long way in giving staff more control and responsibility for their own work. Team leaders can improve motivation at all levels in the organization by applying some of the following ideas.

- Allow the individual member of staff to do a better job. Rules and regulations, of both internal and external nature, may place restrictions on the employee. Look at these restrictions or barriers to motivation and see if they can be curtailed to allow more empowerment of the individual.
- Remove any parts of the job that represent ineffective work. Many tasks we do day-to-day are demotivational because they contain elements that do not make sense, their logic is not visible or they lead to no positive effect at all. The best people to tell you about their jobs are the staff themselves. Encourage challenge and see if certain tasks can be eliminated or at least simplified.
- Encourage members of staff to comment openly on the work they are doing. Staff like to air their grievances and, although you may not be able to change a situation because of company policy or legislation, airing areas of concern and then debating them is motivational, as the employees can at least understand the position they are stuck with.
- Make the job interesting. All work has a particular mixture of the enjoyable and the boring. Problems arise when the job is perceived to have more boring than

satisfying content. It may be necessary to rearrange work between various team members so that the more boring content is more evenly distributed. In one large insurance company in the United Kingdom, data input clerks are given more interesting work after the lunch break. Job sharing is successful if carefully planned and explained.

- Structure the job to enable the employee to monitor her own performance. Some jobs are so constructed that employees are self-regulatory, i.e., they can actually see how they are doing. However, many jobs do not have this facility and in this case regular feedback from the boss is necessary.

- Make sure that the job provides staff with opportunities for organizational growth, i.e., promotion and/or personal growth. Some jobs are what used to be called "dead-end jobs," offering people little or no chance for individual recognition, or for learning and advancement.

- Supervise staff only at the necessary level, and let them have the maximum freedom a job will allow. Regular checking and very tight supervision may be very demotivational for the member of staff. It often stifles initiative and frustrates the employee. People are always capable of taking responsibility for their own jobs with adequate training and management encouragement.

- Make sure that your feedback to members of staff is effective. Unfortunately feedback on individual and team performance is not always handled very well. One of the influencing skills necessary for the modern manager and team leader is to know how not to embarrass people or put them on the spot. This would lead to ill will and defense, which in turn would impact upon cooperation and team effort.

- It is very important for individuals and teams to feel that the job is worth doing. This is often a matter of perception. Never let employees think that they are only cogs in the wheel and that whatever they do will make no difference to the business. All jobs, all people, have value; make sure this is communicated.

- Through delegation and empowerment, make employees accountable for their own work. This will give them a sense of responsibility and recognition.

- Give people a whole job of work to do, not just part of it. Nothing is more irritating and demotivational than doing a job part way and then having to hand it over to someone else to complete. This is particularly so if the member of staff does not trust the work of the recipient of his work.

- Give staff more authority to do their job. Empower them through the budgetary system to be responsible for ordering and allocation of resources. Don't tie their hands. This will give employees responsibility, achievement, and recognition.

- Lift the lid on secrecy. Allow your staff to see all the key performance indicators or reports on how they are doing. This will enhance their recognition motivator.

- Slowly, and through training, introduce new and more difficult tasks as you discard the more routine and boring jobs. This will not only give staff a sense of job security, because you are replacing old work with better new work, but will motivate them through personal growth and development.

- Make sure staff are given specific and specialized tasks within their skill base. This will motivate them through growth and the opportunity for advancement. Allow some of your staff to develop expertise in allocated areas.
- Introduce cross training. This will give more cover and more job interest, and help with job security. Cross training, especially in transferable skills, means more personal growth and the opportunity for advancement.

Motivation encourages people to take control of their own lives and at the same time treats them as the professional people they are. That is what your boss has demanded for himself. You have the right to demand it for yourself, and a duty to deliver it to others in your teams and your workplace.

Index

NOTES

NOTES

NOTES

NOTES

NOTES

NOTES